# GRACIOUS GHOSTS
## OF CHEYENNE

JILL POPE

Published by Haunted America
A Division of The History Press
Charleston, SC
www.historypress.com

All images are from author's collection unless otherwise noted.

First published 2021

Manufactured in the United States

ISBN 9781540248169

Library of Congress Control Number: 2021934126

*Notice*: The information in this book is true and complete to the best of our knowledge. It is offered without guarantee on the part of the author or The History Press. The author and The History Press disclaim all liability in connection with the use of this book.

# CONTENTS

# CONTENTS

# INTRODUCTION

*We have always held to the hope, the belief, the conviction*
*that there is a better life, a better world, beyond the horizon.*
*—Franklin D. Roosevelt*

There is a dark connotation to the word *paranormal*. The definition of *paranormal* is an experience that can't be obviously explained scientifically. After years of collecting stories, I know that many paranormal experiences are coming from loved ones, spirit guides and angels and not from anything dark. This book is on the lighter side of the supernatural, as it's a compilation of *positive experiences* that come from another realm. Many spirits just like to be seen and acknowledged but have no evil intent. In fact, they are generally spending time around us as a loving gesture, to provide guidance and be around their loved ones, to watch their children and grandchildren grow and experience life and guide us when we are struggling, giving us reassuring touches.

Spirits of loved ones are often seen shortly after their passing. They want to check on their family and let them know that they are still around, continuing to attend important events such as birthdays, graduations and weddings. The veil between these worlds is very thin. Don't be hurt if you didn't feel or see a loved one after their passing—sometimes they are just figuring out how to navigate in their new realm.

Spirits will come help people to cross over in their final hours on Earth. Medical professionals know that the terminally ill often speak to family members who are dead in their final hours because they truly can see them.

# INTRODUCTION

Pay attention, as our loved ones leave us subtle messages and reminders that they are near. *Love notes*.

Many people profess that angels are everywhere among us during good and bad times and are here to assist us and bring hope. Angels can appear in a white luminous form or can look just like any human. If this is true, you may have passed one on the street today. Our family and friends also look over us and guide us.

The book is divided into three parts.

Part I of this book relays my personal experiences with entities from the other side. I share many personal encounters with you in these pages. Some people are more open to accepting messages from beyond and receptive to their intuition and senses. They see, hear, feel and acknowledge spirit clearly and more effortlessly than the general public. When people are closed off to the idea of spirit, they may not notice the subtle things spirits do to get our attention. Spirits are in tune with people's energy. If a person is close-minded to the idea of the afterlife, it repels the spirit. Why would a soul waste its energy on a person who would deny its existence, miss the signs or brush it off? Their efforts are much better spent on someone who will sense and acknowledge them.

We all have our own talents. Some people have mathematical brains, some are born with incredible artistic talents and others have intuitive gifts. While everyone can read, meditate and learn to develop their intuition to a higher degree, it comes naturally to others. I feel a connection with spirits—I think they like me because I tell their stories.

Part II of this book includes stories of spirits that have stayed or often visit the home where they resided in their human lives. They make themselves known to the current residents, but not in threatening ways. These spirits can be responsive to what is happening and can interact with you. The idea of residual energy comes from the theory that the energy from past human activity can remain, especially in areas where there were lots of people and intense emotion. This is why you hear of so many stories of apparitions at the site of the 1863 Battle of Gettysburg in Pennsylvania. There was so much emotion from the battle that the energy is literally imprinted in the space, much like a tape recording that keeps replaying. Residual energy cannot interact, as it is nonresponsive.

# INTRODUCTION

The stories I recount here were shared with me by the individuals who experienced them. To respect people's privacy, I have changed the names in many of the stories.

PART III OF THIS book discusses businesses with friendly spirits. I can say with a clear conscience that nearly all the historic buildings along the downtown main street Lincolnway in Cheyenne, Wyoming, have paranormal activity. Lincolnway is a portion of the original Lincoln Highway, which was the prelude to the interstate highway system. The Lincoln Highway revolutionized travel at a time when the world was converting from horse and buggies to automobiles. There is a marker designating the Lincoln Highway outside the city parking garage at the corner of Lincolnway and Carey Avenue. These markers were originally placed all along the highway, which stretched from New York to San Francisco, but today only four markers remain.

Lincoln Highway marker in Cheyenne, Wyoming.

## INTRODUCTION

Cheyenne was a popular stop for travelers. It boasted the elegant Inter Ocean Hotel at the corner of Lincolnway and Capitol Avenue. It was the richest city per capita in the whole of the United States in the early 1880s, largely due to the cattle industry.

THE MAJORITY OF THESE stories—but not all—transpired in Cheyenne, Wyoming, because this is the city where I work. I write the Halloween Frightseeing Trolley Tour scripts in Cheyenne and have spent a lot of time over the past eighteen years compiling peoples' unexplained events.

I am not repeating any stories that were published in my previous two books—*Haunted Cheyenne* and *Haunted Warren Air Force Base*—but there are a few stories in this book from locations discussed in the previous books. I am continually learning of new paranormal encounters.

When the energy or essence of a person is seen after leaving the physical body, it is referred to as a ghost or spirit. It's a fact that we lose about six ounces in weight upon death, supporting the theory that the spirit leaves the body.[1]

We think of paranormal investigators as a new thing, as it's a big trend in today's culture, but such activity goes way back. The Society for Psychical Research was founded in 1882, and one of its first mandates was investigating hauntings. Much like today, some of the encounters were proven to be false, but not all could be dismissed. Our technology and techniques are more sophisticated today, but even so, many skeptics remain.

# PART I

# My Personal Experiences

*Everything you have ever wanted is on the other side of fear.*
*—George Adair*

CHAPTER 1

# PERCEPTION

## INNER VOICES: INTUITION

Do you ever hear a voice from within, a calling, an urge on the direction of your life? Have you ever thought, "Something is telling me to do this"? This begs the question: is it your subconscious you hear, or something more? Could the voice that gives guidance be originating from a source beyond your own thoughts or control? Hearing voices may not be a sign of insanity but rather someone or something from beyond this realm giving you direction. Depending on your belief system, this guidance can be attributed to different things.

Joan of Arc followed that internal voice, and she is considered a religious martyr. Joan was born a peasant girl in what is now France. Professing divine guidance and with no military training, she led the French army to several important victories during the Hundred Years' War. At the age of nineteen, Joan was captured and burned at the stake for witchcraft and heresy. The Roman Catholic Church canonized her as a saint in 1920. The perception of the community members who killed her diverged greatly from the church's viewpoint.[2]

President Lincoln was in tune with his sixth sense. He dreamed of his death a few days prior to his assassination. On that fateful day of April 15, 1865, Lincoln summoned his cabinet, saying, "Gentlemen, before long you will have important news. I have had a dream, the same dream that I have had three times before." Within hours, the devastating news raced through the city: President Lincoln had been shot at Ford's Theatre.[3]

Following the murder, his spirit was reportedly seen at the White House. Winston Churchill slept in the Lincoln Room, where he saw Lincoln's spirit. President Teddy Roosevelt and First Lady Grace Coolidge both reported seeing a tall, gangly figure in several rooms of the residence. Others have reported seeing Lincoln's shadow in the Oval Office window.

This book tells of spirits that visit and guide us. There are many empaths in the world, and I am one of them. I physically feel and absorb the emotions of those around me. We all do this to some extent. It can prove difficult to be in crowded spaces such as an airport—it's overwhelming to absorb everyone's emotions and anxiety. I don't claim to be a psychic medium and won't be hanging my medium shingle out, although I do occasionally have wonderful experiences and insights that come to me from another dimension—heaven, as many of you know it. We *all* receive messages from spirits, but we don't always know or understand where they are coming from. We can experience it as intuition, a gut feeling or even a bright idea. It's a true gift to be able to see or hear a spirit before you. If there is not a negative feeling when you see an apparition, then by all means embrace the experience.

I chose to write this book mainly due to the numerous experiences I have personally had. The veil between our world as we know it and the afterlife is very thin. I hope that anyone struggling with the loss of a loved one can find comfort from these stories and the understanding that those souls that have passed over are not far away. They can see and hear you.

A few of these experiences are hard to share because they are very personal, but I've been guided to put it all out there. I hope that my friends and family will embrace the words.

## CHAPTER 2

# REFLECTIONS

*To see a world in a grain of sand and heaven in a wildflower/Hold infinity in the palm of your hand and eternity in an hour.*
*—William Blake*

## UPRISING

A story from my ancestors was passed down to me. My great-great-grandmother Frances Jaeger lived in St. Peter, Minnesota, in 1862. It was a different time. The Dakota Native Americans, more commonly referred to as the Sioux (which I've read can be a derogatory term), were at odds with the federal government. While I don't choose to get political here, it is no secret that the white man, especially those in the government, mistreated the American Indians. This treatment led to an uprising that began in New Ulm, Minnesota, just twenty-five miles from where my family lived. The next five months of turmoil were devastating. Many settlers and Native Americans died during that time.

One afternoon, Frances and her two young daughters were home. She had just baked fresh bread, and the kitchen's aroma was wonderful. As Frances placed the loaf of bread on the counter, she glanced out the window and saw two Native American braves coming down her driveway. Terrified, she dropped to her knees in prayer. How was she going to keep her daughters safe? Frances relayed that she felt a protective spirit come from above and surround her. She continued praying as the men burst into her home. Frances stood, took the loaf of freshly baked bread from her counter and offered it to the Dakota men, who ate it greedily. Then they turned and left without harming Frances or her daughters. This was considered a miracle.

# FAMILY ROOTS

My great-grandmother Rogers had been bedridden for a while. My great-grandpa Neal had already passed away, so their daughter, my grandma Beth, took her mother in and lovingly looked after her. I was just three years old, and I don't know much about her illness, but I believe she was near the age of ninety. I can still recall her lying in her bed, with her stark white hair.

Oddly, I also remember rubbing Huskers Corn Lotion (in the bottle with the yellow and green label) on her feet whenever we stopped over at my grandparents' home. She found it comforting; my mother instructed me about how to tenderly massage the bottoms of her feet the whole time.

It was relayed to me years later that just moments before her death, she sat straight up in bed, with her arms extended, and said "Nealie" with a joyful smile. Her beloved husband, Neal, was there to greet her and help her transition to the other side. What a comfort for Grandmother Beth to know they were together.

# IS THAT YOU?

My uncle Bob had a relative on the other side of his family named Dee. Dee was widowed, but shortly after her husband's passing, she awoke in the middle of the night. Once her sleep fog subsided, she realized that a man was standing at the end of her bed. It was her husband's spirit. While I don't know what they said to each other, Dee did tell my uncle that they had communicated, and she felt much relief and solace from his visit.

## MET HIS MAKER

I was married at the tender age of eighteen, head over heels in love with my high school sweetheart, Jamie. My husband was very close to his family. We found his paternal grandparents especially endearing. They were both small in stature, and Grandpa went by the name "Shorty." He was such a feisty character; I smile at his memory every time my mind goes to him.

Shorty spent most of his days in Cheyenne. He was a retired blue-collar worker in the bus transportation industry. While he was a bit ornery, those who knew him realized that his bark was way worse than his bite. He was an active senior who kept his home and grounds in top-notch condition. He had been married more than fifty years to Mary, and they provided a nice haven for their kids and grandkids. Mary was the perfect balance for Shorty—she loved him and kept him in line the best anyone could.

Mary was taken aback one summer morning during breakfast when Shorty announced that this was his last day on this earth. "Don't be ridiculous, Shorty, your health is fine," Mary retorted. There had been no indication that he was ill. Less than thirty minutes later, Shorty lay unconscious on the kitchen floor. The paramedics were unable to revive him; his death was labeled a stroke. We were all devastated at this unexpected loss. The question remains: how did Grandpa Shorty know that he was going to meet his maker that day?

## GREAT-GRANDPA'S FINAL VISIT

The year was 1983. Jamie and I were a young married couple, and we were so very proud of our beautiful blond-haired, blue-eyed baby girl, Heather. She had been born four months earlier. Heather was the first grandchild on Jamie's side of the family, and she received an abundance of loving adoration.

One sad day, we were notified that Jamie's maternal grandfather, Herman, had passed on. While he was up in years, everyone grieved deeply. After a day of gathering with the family and friends at his funeral, the three of us returned home. I tucked baby Heather into her crib with her favorite blankie and yellow musical teddy bear. We climbed into bed, exhausted after the long, emotional day. Just as we had drifted off to sleep, we were awakened by the sounds of Heather's musical teddy bear. Occasionally, when she would roll over, the bear might play a note or two, but this was different—somehow the bear had been fully wound, and the song was playing from beginning to end. Jamie and I looked at each other knowingly, and we both realized that her great-grandfather was visiting her before moving on. We could hear her cooing in response to her special visitor. The experience warmed our hearts and helped us move forward.

# EARLY TO RISE

I am fortunate to have grown up near both sets of my grandparents. I was in my forties when I lost my maternal grandparents, first Grandpa Bill and next Grandma Beth.

About two weeks before Grandma Beth passed away, there was one of those events that many would call unexplainable. My aunt and uncle, a few friends and their minister and his wife were in Grandma's hospital room with her. They had brought her yellow roses. Grandma began speaking to family members who were no longer with us. She said, "Steven, please hold these flowers for Grandma." We had lost her grandson Steven to cancer a few years earlier. Grandma got a happy expression on her face and said, "Sweetheart," which they all knew was her deceased husband, Bill; they were such a loving couple. This was followed by a medical episode, and the nurses rushed in. They all heard Beth say, "Why do I have to go back?"

Grandma lived that day, but she told my aunt and uncle that she had been in heaven and that it is so wonderful. She said that she had seen her beloved Bill, her parents, her sister and so many family and friends. She smiled broadly as she shared the experience with them. I'm not sure why Grandma Beth needed to stay here on earth another two weeks; maybe she needed to say some things to people before transitioning, or maybe it was to share this beautiful story with us so we could deal with her death easier.

# I Give My Heart to You

*The best and most beautiful things in the world cannot be seen or even touched—they must be felt with the heart.*
*Helen Keller*

On August 1, 1981, I married Jamie. We had dated for two years and had a strong, easy love. I say "easy" because we just didn't have to constantly explain ourselves—we were generally on the same page and just got each other. We enjoyed a simple life. We did not have a lot of money, but we got by. In 1989, we purchased a charming little house near Holliday Park. We had two beautiful children, a girl and a boy. Perfect.

Jamie enrolled in college about ten years into the marriage, majoring in engineering. I respected him so very much because he worked during the day while remaining a very involved father. He was the PTO president and assistant softball coach. Jamie took accelerated college classes on the weekend and never did his homework until after the kids were tucked into bed. Needless to say, he survived on very little sleep but still excelled in everything he did.

It was a proud day when he graduated with an engineering degree. He was already working at the refinery, and this would open up doors for advancement. He was soon promoted, and life was great. I also had a good job. We could breathe financially now. We had done some remodeling to our little cottage home. The world was bright.

In 1994, after being together for fifteen years, which was half of my life, Jamie was killed in a car accident. It was devastating. I didn't know how to live without him. The moment Jamie passed away, I internally knew. I had been dozing, a bit unnerved because he wasn't home. I sat straight up and looked around, feeling great anxiety; I knew things weren't right. I couldn't go back to sleep or do anything because of the overwhelming anxiety that I couldn't explain. Then the police officers arrived, and my worst fear was confirmed.

One of Jamie's best friends from childhood told me that Jamie had come to him the following night. He saw his apparition, and it had terrified him, although I know Jamie was telling him that he was still around and that it would be okay.

# RINGING IN THE NEW YEAR

The previous New Year's Eve, we had gathered at our friends Pam and Frank's home with friends Carol and Chuck to ring in the new year together. As midnight neared, Jamie uncorked the champagne bottle with a bang; the cork rocketed from the bottle into the ceiling tile with force, tearing through the tile. We all laughed cheerfully. We replaced the ceiling tile the next day.

Chuck was on the telephone breaking the devastating news about Jamie to Frank when something incredible happened. The very ceiling tile that we had replaced fell inexplicably from the ceiling and landed at Frank's feet. He stood there speechless.

# GOING ON

Early one morning, one month after Jamie's passing and after I had returned to work, I sat at my desk as an elementary school secretary with my hands wrapped around a warm cup of coffee. I sat there with the lights off, arriving to work a half hour before the teachers arrived each day. As I sat there alone in the dark, I was struggling through my grief, reflecting on my tremendous loss and trying to gather the strength to face the day. This was a sad and terrifying period of life for me and my children. I just didn't know how to carry on without Jamie.

Sitting there, as I was reflecting on how I missed my soul mate, feeling a huge hole in the core of my being, the computer printer spit out a sheet of paper. This was odd because I had not touched my computer—I had not even turned it on.

I looked over at the dot matrix printer and ripped off the page that had come out. My heart lunged when I saw a single character on the page: a heart. A note from my love. A sign that he was there with me. This single symbol on a sheet of paper really helped me hang on. I still treasure that sheet of paper.

# Being Neighborly

Prior to Jamie's passing, we were living in our charming little blue cottage home. We had befriended our neighbors, an elderly couple. There was hardly a day where we did not interact with Ted and Paulette. They were very special to us. There were a few events where angels or spirits intervened for their protection.

One night, in the middle of the night around 2:00 a.m., I suddenly awoke with a strong feeling to get out of bed and survey things. I walked through our living room and noticed the faint odor of smoke. Continuing through the house, I didn't find any cause for alarm, but I still felt unnerved. As I passed the kitchen window, I noticed a light on in the neighbors' garage. "That's unusual," I thought. Ted was not one to leave a light on. I stopped, and then I saw an ember float down and realized the garage was on fire. I dashed to the bedroom and woke Jamie up. He was on the fire brigade for the refinery and had completed firefighting training at Texas A&M. I ran and woke up Ted and Paulette in fear that the fire would spread to the house. Then I called 911 while Jamie went to work extinguishing the fire. Most of the garage was burned, but they were able to get the fire out before it spread to the house.

Another evening, just before bedtime, I began to feel really sick. It hit me fast and hard, all the classic symptoms of the flu. There was no way I could go in to work in the morning. I ached all over, had a bad headache and spent most of the night and the following morning in the restroom.

All of a sudden, all my symptoms were just gone. I sat on the couch in wonderment. I went from super sick to feeling fine in a matter of minutes. I had never recovered so rapidly in the past. Right then, I heard a knock on the door. I opened the door to find a frantic Paulette. "Please help me, something is really wrong with my grandson."

I ran to their house. Matt, their twenty-year-old grandson, was conscious but unresponsive. I called 911, and the ambulance came. Matt was hospitalized; he had suffered a nervous breakdown. I was so glad I had been home to help Paulette and Matt. Ted was out of town that day, and Paulette needed help and emotional support.

There was no doubt in my mind that there had been an intervention from beyond in both these situations.

# SONG REQUEST

My sister Peggy and her husband, Dale, lived in Cheyenne, Wyoming, for many years but then moved back to Minnesota, where we had all grown up. When my husband, Jamie, was still alive, the four of us hung out a lot. We watched football every Sunday during the season, and we were on a pool league together. Sunday dinners were often enjoyed together at our parents' home. There was a neighborhood bar that we all liked to frequent, and we were friends with the owner. This is where many of our pool league games were played.

After they had moved back to Minnesota and after we lost Jamie, Peggy and Dale came to Cheyenne for a visit. We met up at that same bar to reminisce. As we settled in around our table, the band announced, "The next song is dedicated to Dale from Jamie." We all looked up at the same time with shocked expressions. It felt like more than just a coincidence. The song that followed was "You Picked a Fine Time to Leave Me Lucille," which had been one of the guys' favorite singalong songs that was popular and would play while we were shooting pool.

# VISION

This is a story I have not shared with many people. One of those moments in life that hits you in your core.

The year was 2004. I had a good friend, Christine, who had become a reiki practitioner. This was before reiki was "cool," and most of us had never heard of it. She needed a logo for her business, and since I was a friend and an artist, she asked me to create a logo for her. I was honored.

Once she set up her table, she invited me over for a free reiki session. Although I wasn't too sure what it involved, I was excited to give it a try. I climbed up on the massage table, feeling completely relaxed. Christine explained that reiki is an ancient hands-on healing exercise dealing with people's energy flow. The practice dates back many thousand years, even before the time of Christ or Buddha. *Reiki* is a Japanese word meaning "universal life force."

It's a scientific fact that everything is energy. Human beings are composed of energy. Energy flow is similar to radio waves—they are there, but we can't see them. A reiki practitioner channels the client's energy to help it flow freely.

As I comfortably lay there, a strong image came into my head, and each time I tried to clear it from my head it returned. So, I told Christine, "This is really weird, but I keep seeing a coffin in my mind." She felt that since we were clearing energies, I was just releasing some of the grief that my body had stored from losing Jamie. Reiki helps release emotional baggage. While that was reasonable, something inside me knew that it wasn't correct.

I did feel relaxed and rejuvenated after the reiki session despite the vision. The next night, I had just settled into bed when I got a call from my stepdad. My mother had been sent to the hospital by ambulance. We rushed there only to learn that she had suffered a brain aneurism and her brain had been flooded with blood. There was no brain activity.

I knew that this was what my vision with a casket had been about. It was a premonition of what was to come. I saw Christine outside the church at my mother's funeral. We just hugged and were both overwhelmed by what had transpired.

I am now a reiki master myself, although more so on paper, as I haven't had much practical experience at this time. Most people who receive reiki do not get visions. As I said earlier, I sometimes receive messages from the other side. It happened during a reiki session because I was so relaxed that the meditative state allowed the message to come through.

# CHAPTER 3
# HOME SWEET HOME

## CURRENT DAY

*There is nothing so powerful as the truth, and often nothing so strange.*
*—Daniel Webster*

M oving forward more than a decade, after a long healing process I am blessed to be remarried to Darin, a wonderful guy with integrity. We bought a rural home with the Rocky Mountains in our backyard and a dairy farm across the street. The views are tremendous, as is the quiet lifestyle.

## REMOTELY

I was thoroughly enjoying a day off work and had decided to sort through and organize all my jewelry. This was going to take a while, as I love baubles. I went to turn on the bedroom television to listen to while doing this task, but as usual, I could not locate the remote control. I was certain it was on our bed; one by one, I pulled back each blanket and sheet. No remote. I wasn't sure which of the buttons to push on the TV itself and didn't want to mess up the settings, as I'm not known for my technology skills.

I finished making the bed, taking my time to smooth out and line up the blankets perfectly. Still no remote. I looked under the bed and all around the bedroom. Not wanting to waste any more time, I ventured out to the living room to get that remote. Returning to the bedroom, I immediately saw the bedroom TV's remote control lying in the center of the freshly made bed. I was a bit shocked. I just sat on the bench for about five minutes staring at the remote and taking in what had just transpired.

After regaining my composure, I thanked the spirit for helping me and went forward with my project.

# What Chord?

I was having difficulty sleeping. I lay tossing and turning on the couch in the dead silence of the night when I was startled by a loud, high-pitched sound that rang out through our living room. It sounded like someone hit a piano key, but we don't own a piano.

I was trying to come up with a reasonable explanation when another sound rang out. This one was in a lower key and had a more resounding tone. That's when I realized that it was a strum from the guitar that was leaning against the wall about six feet from me. I jumped up and flipped the light on. Considering the sounds, I wondered if possibly a mouse could have come in contact with the guitar since we do live out in the country. I moved the guitar around and thumped it with my fingers but could not duplicate the sound without actually plucking the string with my fingernail. There was no way a mouse could do that—twice.

# Step Up

My husband, Darin, and I, along with our adult son, Brady, were outside on the front deck one lovely fall evening. They were enjoying a cigar and taking in the mountain views before the weather turned. I went inside for a moment. When I was headed back out to the deck, I noticed that our dog Emmitt was going up the stairs. He is a Westie, so not too big. It was unusual for the dog to leave my husband's side unless he was chasing a ball or a rabbit. Suddenly, Emmitt jumped down about six feet from one of the middle steps to the tile floor below. This was quite a plunge for the little fella. He scrambled for his footing and sprinted off as fast as his little legs would take him.

Giggling, I said, "Whatcha doing, Emmitt, you goof." Then I turned and looked up the staircase, where I clearly saw the silhouette of a man ascending the steps. "Oh, you're hanging out with Brady," I said. I turned and was headed to the front door when I noticed a really odd look on my husband's face. Then I realized that Brady was still sitting on the deck bench. I turned and looked back up the stairs, but no one was there now. I stammered, "But, but I just saw you on the steps." Darin said, "I saw someone on the steps too. I thought it was you until you spoke to the dog and I realized you were in the kitchen and not on the steps." It was nighttime, so I hadn't seen vivid colors really when I looked up the unlit staircase to the dark second floor, but it was a defined outline of a man wearing shorts with a baseball cap on.

A few hours later, both the dogs, Mortimer and Emmitt, began to react at the stair landing. Their fur bristled, they growled and they crept backward about ten feet, cowering as they began to tremble. It took nearly an hour to calm them down.

The next night, while everyone was fast asleep, the television in our bedroom suddenly turned on, with the volume blaring. Our spirit was making his presence known.

Darin had never bought into the idea of ghosts, but after seeing the apparition, he admitted that this wasn't his first encounter in the home. He said that there had been numerous times in the basement when the ghost would throw the ball for the dogs. They would bring it back and drop it on the floor, and as soon as Darin would look away, the ball would travel swiftly back down the hallway and the dogs would run to fetch it.

About six months later, we had a house guest. In the morning over coffee, she inquired as to why we had not told her that we had a ghost. "Oh my gosh, what happened?" I asked. She relayed that she had been awakened during the night; her bed was shaking, and there was a large, dark silhouette lurking near the doorway. She was petrified and stayed frozen in the bed until morning. This was odd because we've never felt intimidated by our spirit.

# KARAOKE

It was a few days after Christmas 2016. I was tidying up the kitchen. I finished and walked about ten steps into the living room. It's an open-concept floor plan with no wall between the rooms, just a breakfast counter.

Something on the television had caught my attention, and I stood there watching for a bit. Then I noticed a noise coming from around the stove. I wondered if my husband had put the tea kettle on, but I knew I would have seen and heard him come into the room. The odd noise continued, so I walked back over to the stove. The fan had been turned on. The fan dial has tight tension and does not turn easily. No one had been in the kitchen when the fan turned on, at least nobody I could see.

This happened again just the other day while I was working on this book, four years later. Our lives are filled with interactions from the other side. I believe it's because I tell their stories.

The next day, I was at work, but Darin was home. He was in the kitchen when he heard blaring music coming from another part of the house near the extra bathroom. He couldn't figure out how music could be playing, as he was the only person in the house. He walked through the sunroom to the spare bathroom. The music stopped. He looked around but didn't find anything.

Darin went back to the kitchen, and a minute or so later he clearly heard loud music again. Really confused, he walked back toward the sound. Again it stopped as he stood outside the bathroom. He was really unnerved at this point. He went back to the kitchen, and wouldn't you know it, the music started up again. This time, it didn't stop when he walked toward it.

My art studio is beside the bathroom. There is an old karaoke machine with a radio component that was blaring. We hadn't turned it on in five years. Darin didn't even know it was there until that moment.

Later that day, around 5:30 p.m., Darin was in his home office when our dog Emmitt walked into the room with the kitchen towel that had been folded and was sitting up on the kitchen island countertop. The towel was perfectly draped across the dog's back like a saddle blanket. Emmitt is a Westie, which is a short, stocky breed. He could not reach the countertop even if there was a big steak up there to tempt him, much less place the towel perfectly over his back.

# ROOMMATE

Brad, a friend, lived with us for a while. After about a week at the house, Brad came into the dining room with a puzzled look on his face. Darin and I were already seated at the table. I asked what was wrong. He asked if we had ghosts! I said, "Well, yes, we've had some things happen." He went on to explain that he thought Darin had just walked up right beside him and said hello in his ear, but when he turned around to respond, no one was there. We were both in the dining room. Brad had heard and felt a presence beside him and was a bit shook up by it.

A few weeks later, Brad was walking through our sunroom, and a voice in his ear said, "I'm staying awhile," as if it enjoyed taunting him. These instances happened frequently to Brad during his stay. Honestly, I believe that the spirit enjoyed messing with him just for the reaction.

# INTERACTIONS

One night, I had just crawled into bed and was drifting off when my husband called my name. I groggily went out to the living room. My husband was giving me that *look*, and I knew that something paranormal had happened. While he is into UFO and Sasquatch sightings, he never believed in ghosts. Life with me, though, has made it undeniable for him.

There was just the two of us living there, as we are empty nesters; it was late and the house was quiet. Darin had been sitting on the couch watching the television when an antique metal stirrup that hung on the wall flew about seven feet across the room and landed on his foot. Simultaneously, a book about ghosts flew out of the bookshelf and hit the floor. I think our spirit wanted to be acknowledged.

While writing this book in March 2020, I closed my document but left my laptop turned on while cooking dinner. We were sitting down at the table for dinner when all of a sudden we could hear music. The television was turned on, but we heard more sounds coming from the sunroom. Not again, I thought! I went out to the sunroom, and my computer was playing a YouTube video. There were also three other tabs open on the computer that I had not opened. We don't have a cat, and it was just my husband and me in the house, so we could not explain this away.

I feel, hear or see spirits in my home nearly every day, but we cohabitate well. The man who previously lived in our home passed away from Lou Gehrig's disease. It's possible that he has chosen to hang around, but I believe that a lot of the energy is our deceased family members.

CHAPTER **4**

# PERSONAL ENCOUNTERS
# OF THE PARANORMAL KIND

## ISSIE'S IN THE ATTIC

I boldly walked into the Romsa Law Offices in Cheyenne, Wyoming, one day without an appointment and asked if they had ghosts! The offices are established in a wonderful historic home on Pioneer Avenue. I am always looking for new material for the Annual Halloween Trolley Frightseeing Tours. Mr. Romsa was quite nice about the intrusion and said, "Well, yes we do. There's a little old lady in the attic."

When he began telling me of the home's history, I recognized the prominent names of those who had once lived there. Jochim Arp was a founding father of Cheyenne. He owned a very successful hardware store in the 1800s. There is an elementary school in town named after this pioneer family. Arp's wife, Anna, died shortly after the birth of their fifth child, Anna Christine. His eldest daughter helped raise the other children and ran the household. When she got engaged, her father built this beautiful home for her and her new husband.

A man named Doran Lummis married the youngest Arp daughter, Anna. The Lummises are an esteemed ranching family in Cheyenne. Their daughter, Cynthia Lummis, is currently a U.S. senator for Wyoming. The home remained in the Arp-Lummis family for many years to come.

Mr. Romsa, introducing himself as Matt, kindly gave me a tour of the home. He appreciates the home's history, and I think he enjoyed the

Romsa Law Office in 2020. Jochim Arp built the home.

supernatural aspects as well. We ascended the narrow creaky steps to the attic. Even though it is an unfinished attic, it was a surprisingly light and uplifting space that felt comfortable to me. It had angled walls, as most attics do; there were file boxes stacked up, but it was otherwise empty.

Matt said that he and his wife have seen the spirit of an older woman up there several times and that the Lummises spoke of her fondly. They call her Issie, but he's not sure why. They hear unusual noises in the home at times, and they hear doors shut on their own accord. There has never been any negative activity.

## ELEVATOR RIDE

We have a polite elevator spirit in the depot building where I work that likes to interact with us. On a few occasions when I was in the depot lobby and it was quiet, with not a soul around, the elevator doors parted when I approached, but I was still about ten feet back. I always say "thank you" and get in.

A depot custodian has had the same experience. He was always the first person to arrive at the depot very early in the morning. He said that when

Cheyenne Historic Depot lobby, 2020.

he arrived and headed toward the elevator, the doors often opened for him before he reached it, way before he could push the buttons. There were times when he was in the building alone at really early hours and heard the elevator go to the basement, but there were no other people in the building to call the elevator to the basement—just the basement ghouls.

Debbie is quite often the first one to work in the morning, and she often has to wait for the elevator to come up from the basement. She was wondering how it got down there to start with. We were wondering if somehow it just drops down a floor during the night, but frankly the thought of that scares me more than a ghost.

## STAIRCASE

In August 2018, I held a Spirit Spree Paranormal Conference along with the Kindred Spirits group out of northern Colorado. The Spirit Spree was held at the Cheyenne Historic Depot. I took a group of paranormal enthusiasts down to the basement, where the history of the building is evident.

The 1886 depot is a magnificent Romanesque stone building with a tall clock tower. I often say that I wish the walls could talk—you literally feel

Cheyenne Historic Depot basement staircase apparition.

the history dripping from the walls. Sometimes the spirits do reveal bits of its past.

Some of the people in the group were taking pictures, and others had EMF readers, dowsing rods or other investigation equipment. I was standing beside Kate, and as she had not ever been involved in any paranormal investigation, I suggested that she just snap some photos on her phone while we were down there.

Later, Kate scrolled through her photos. She was stunned to see the apparition of a woman. We stared at her cellphone screen, scrutinizing the clear image of legs and feet perched on the old wooden staircase. Had I not been standing beside Kate when she took the picture, I would have been hard pressed to believe that this photo was for real. I knew that no one was on the staircase—in this realm—when the photo was taken. There is more than meets the eye down here.

## Depot Basement

A group of paranormal investigators from the Kindred Spirits Society of the Rockies, based in Longmont, Colorado, were at the Spirit Spree event. After I showed them Kate's photo, they excitedly set their equipment up on the basement staircase. A flashlight and a ghost box were responsive here, meaning that when the team asked questions aloud, the light beam flashed accordingly and the ghost box displayed words.

The team had the sense of a woman here. They felt the apparition was someone that had passed through the area but not necessarily lived in Cheyenne. The words *school* and *poetry* came up on the ghost box. They confirmed with flashlight response that the woman was a schoolteacher and taught her students poetry. The woman was not married, nor did she have any children of her own.

A few years earlier, Gina, another depot employee, shared her story with me. Gina was not frightened in the depot basement, although she has experienced a kindred spirit there. When she stepped out of the elevator onto the narrow walkway winding through the dark shadows of the basement, she heard a woman's voice humming, a beautiful voice that sounded happy. Gina spoke out, "Who's here?" There was no answer. Gina slowly crept down the walkway, and the humming continued. In her mind, she could picture a woman twirling and dancing about, but she saw no one.

After the experience, she came to me to share her lovely story. Then, in the coming months, she stopped into my office a few times to say that she continued to interact with the female spirit nearly every time she went to the basement. Gina had been a performer and singer in her own life, which is why she believed this female spirit related to her. She cherished the experiences.

I speculate that this is the same woman in apparition photo on the stairs. I am curious to know how she is connected to the depot. Just where did she dance her last dance on this earth, on this side of the veil?

## CHAPTER 5

# HEAR THE MESSAGE

*I became insane, with long intervals of horrible sanity.*
*All that we see or seem is but a dream within a dream.*
*—Edgar Allan Poe*

## SAFE TRAVELS

I have an hour drive home from work, and during my commute I listen to audiobooks, enjoying the newest murder mystery, or to a podcast. As I mentioned, I do physically experience entities from the other side. I notice them most often during my commute, as I am quite relaxed, driving mainly on country roads. This will sound strange to many of you, but I know that my angels or spirits are wanting my attention when they tickle my head! I literally feel a strong vibration in my scalp, like my hair follicles are getting electric volts. It starts on the very top of my head and then moves down to my ears and into the ear canals, then my neck and throat. This feels similar to when your hands or feet go to sleep. It's an undeniable stimulus, not subtle, as it used to be.

November 2019 was an especially powerful month empathically. I was driving home one evening and was experiencing this tingling heavier than I ever had. I kept waiting for some image or word or feeling to come to me to help understand what message they had for me, but I just wasn't getting it.

As I neared my home, I turned off a rural gravel road and onto a busy highway that is known to have a lot of car accidents. It was extremely dark in the country, but there was a steady stream of headlights coming my way. After driving this road for the past decade, I have realized that because there are no other external lights besides those of the cars, along with slight curves in the road, it causes an optical illusion, making it appear like cars are heading directly at you in your lane. I think this is one reason why there are so many accidents along this stretch of the road. I panicked on this stretch of the road many times when we first moved to the area, but now I have learned to drive along the white line designating the right edge of my lane where it meets the shoulder. I just hug that line as I drive south and try not to panic as I continue driving. There are a few stops where there are steep drop-offs to the right, so it can be nerve wracking.

On this night, I made it past the area where I normally experience this illusion and was headed south into another curvy area. The tingling continued when, all of a sudden, I realized there *was* a vehicle in my lane—a semi-truck was directly in front of me. With absolutely no panic, I moved my car onto the narrow shoulder, which happened to have a steep drop-off in this spot. The truck narrowly missed me before sliding over sharply in front of a car in the opposing lane. I calmly glided back over into my lane with little fear and said, "Oh, so that's why you are with me tonight. Thank you so very much." It was odd how composed I felt throughout the terrifying situation. I made it safely home that night thanks to my angels and spirit family.

# PART II

# HOME IS WHERE THE HEART IS

*May the Force be with you.*
*—Yoda*

## CHAPTER 6
# HEARTFELT

This section of the book contains stories that were shared with me over the past eighteen years. In order to respect people's privacy, I have changed many of the subject's names and not given specific home addresses. I never want to make anyone uncomfortable sharing their personal stories with me. By sharing these encounters, I hope to help people understand and feel more comfortable with the unexplained events in their lives and the prospect of death.

There are two types of stories in this section. Some are clear heart-based messages to people from their spirit guides, while others are stories where people witnessed remaining energies from another realm or dimension. None of these visitations from the other side of the veil is scary. No harm is intended, although because the experiences are so unexpected and derive from an unknown source, people are often frightened.

## PRIVATE BENJAMIN WALKER

This story was relayed to me by Valerie Martin, trolley guide extraordinaire.

Warren Air Force Base is located in Cheyenne, Wyoming. Originally, this base was Fort D.A. Russell, which was established the very same day as Cheyenne was in 1867. This military post has never shut down and is the longest continually operating military post in the United States.

Captain Egan was working at his desk when Private Benjamin Walker walked into his office. The captain noted that the time was 1700 hours and was surprised that Private Walker would still be on duty. Looking up, Captain Egan noticed that Private Walker was looking rather ashen. He then remembered the private was supposed to be on a flight and said, "What are you doing here?" Private Walker just turned and walked out of the office. Captain Egan sat mulling the strange behavior. Minutes later, the captain received a telephone call informing him of a plane crash in which Private Walker was killed. Ironically, Private Walker's watch had stopped on impact. The watch read 1700 hours.

## CHAPTER 7
# SNAPSHOTS OF LIFE

## PHOTO OPPORTUNITY

A mother and her six-month-old granddaughter posed for a picture at a family gathering in Cheyenne. As they reviewed the photos, they realized that the woman's grandfather appeared in the photo with his daughter and great-granddaughter. However, the man had been dead for twelve years. Our loved ones keep tabs on us after they pass. They are aware of the happenings in our lives and are there to celebrate with us. Love continues.

## CROSS OVER

Pam, a photographer, took a series of five photos consecutively one afternoon. Upon reviewing the pictures, she was intrigued to find an apparition of a man. She was distracted from the photos when her father died three days later. Shortly after they had laid him to rest, Pam's mother noticed the photos on her table and recognized the apparition in the pictures: it was Pam's grandfather. They were comforted by the realization that he was there to help Pam's father cross over, welcoming him to the other side.

## Just Hanging Around

Tightknit siblings Hanna and her brother, Leroy, lived in a house on Twenty-Eighth Street and Central Avenue. When Leroy became terminally ill with cancer, he moved in with his sister so she could look after him. Soon after, he passed away inside their house.

Hanna put the home on the market one year later. The realtor took some promotional photos of the house. Later, the realtor was compelled to show Hanna one of the photos because there was a clear image of her brother, Leroy, standing beside the fireplace in the picture. Hanna said that he was letting her know that he was okay. She often finds pennies—not just one or two but handfuls. She believes this is Leroy giving her his two cents' worth.

## Captain's Image

I reconnected with high school friend Shannon on Facebook, so we go back a few years. When she saw my Facebook posts about the trolley ghost tours and my book *Haunted Cheyenne*, she shared a story with me.

The Captain's house on Cattle Baron's Row, Seventeenth Street.

Shannon's parents owned a large rental home on Seventeenth Street for years. They were the landlords and took special care of the home to preserve its architectural integrity. I remember hanging out there with Shannon and her father while he did a few quick repairs one afternoon in the late 1970s.

The home was built in 1917 and was later subdivided into apartments.[4] During a renovation, Shannon's aunt decided to take a Polaroid photograph of the beautiful mantel that adorned the original fireplace. When the image developed on the photo stock a minute later, they could vividly see the image of an African American woman who appeared to be a maid. Her image appeared in the fireplace opening. A young girl spirit was also revealed in the photograph.

A year later, they took another picture, and incredibly, the same woman and girl appeared, along with a military captain and another male. It looked as though they were posing for a portrait, lost in time.

They learned that the house was built by a captain and that the house behind it on Van Lennon Avenue was the servants' quarters. In that home, an apparition of a young girl is often seen on the staircase. I was told about her from a different lady who had lived there as a child. The girl spirit often played with the children living in the house.

## CHAPTER 8

# HISTORIC HOMES AND CHARACTERS

## NELLIE TAYLOE ROSS

The two-story gabled Ross home was built in 1903 and has been the home to four families, the first of which was Governor William Ross, and his wife, Nellie Tayloe Ross. After William died while in office, a special election was held, and his wife, Nellie, was voted in as the nation's first female governor. Later, she became the first female director of the National Mint.[5]

Their eloquent white colonial home sits just a block from Holliday Park in Cheyenne, Wyoming, on East Seventeenth Street. In speaking with previous residents of this home, I learned that the lights in the front room and dining room would often flicker. They had these rooms rewired, but the flickering continued. They began to say, "Nellie, stop it," and the lights would quit flickering. The toilet would also flush for no reason when no one was in the restroom.

One night, Tanya, a resident, woke up from the noise of her rocking chair moving back and forth. Much to her surprise, she saw a clear apparition of a man in the chair. At first, she assumed it was Governor William Ross, but after looking at old photos, she believes it was Mr. Zackman, another previous tenant.

Three of the four men who have lived in this home died in the master bedroom. The Rosses' infant child was in a buggy on the porch when a gust of wind swept the buggy away and the child perished. The family is buried at Cheyenne Lakeview Cemetery.

Nellie Tayloe Ross, first female governor in the United States, taking the oath of office January 5, 1925. *Wyoming State Archives Collection.*

Nellie Tayloe Ross House, 2020. Nellie was the first female governor in the United States.

# MORRIS HOUSE

As you read through this book or delve into this state's history, you will see why Wyoming is known as the "Equality State." Wyoming was the first state to allow women to vote, to have a female governor, to have a woman on a jury, to have a female judge and even the first state with a professional female athlete. The list goes on.

Esther Hobart Morris is acknowledged by a life-size bronze sculpture of her at the Wyoming state capitol. She was a suffrage advocate and was the first female judge in the nation. Esther owned a cute little cottage home at 2114 Warren Avenue. There is a historical marker in the front yard.

The Morris House Bistro operated successfully in this little home with indoor and outdoor dining space. It was one of my favorite places to eat. The owner became seriously ill, and they ended up closing the bistro, to the great dismay of the community.

Esther had been spotted several times throughout the house turned restaurant. Some employees were there doing a big cleaning project just before the grand opening. A few brought their children, and one of them brought her granddaughter. She hadn't seen the girl for some time, and when the child came into the room, her grandmother asked her where the

Esther Hobart Morris's home on Warren Avenue.

*Left*: Esther Hobart Morris, suffragist. *Wyoming State Archives Collection.*

*Below*: Esther Hobart Morris's historical marker, in her yard.

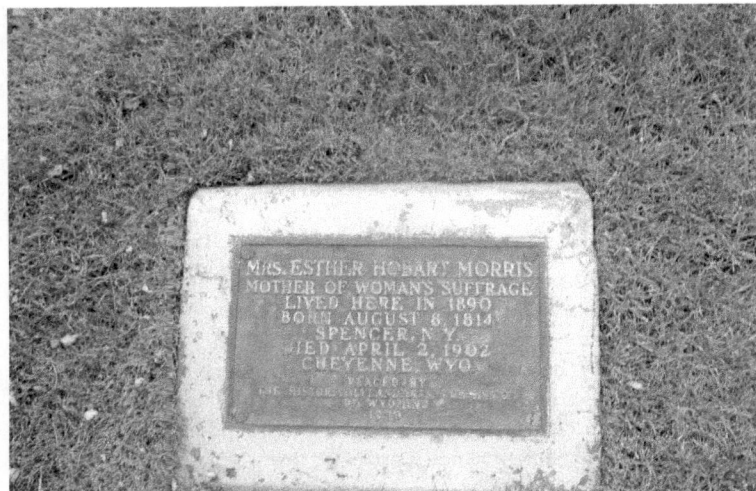

MRS. ESTHER HOBART MORRIS
MOTHER OF WOMAN'S SUFFRAGE
LIVED HERE IN 1890
BORN AUGUST 8, 1814
SPENCER, N.Y.
DIED APRIL 2, 1902
CHEYENNE, WYO.

kids had been. The girl nonchalantly said that she'd been talking to the old lady in the basement. None of the staff was elderly. Of course, they looked in the basement and didn't find anyone.

When they left the bistro, they drove past the front side of the Wyoming capitol building, which was just a few blocks away. The child saw the statue of Esther Hobart Morris and said, "Grandma, that's the lady from your restaurant!"

The restaurant staff told me that when Esther passed away in April 1902, she was lying in her bed for three weeks before she was found. I have not verified this and hope it's not true!

# DAZEE BRISTOL

Dazee Bristol holds a special place in Cheyenne's history. As with many of its women, Dazee was a mover and a shaker. She was an accomplished award-winning journalist. She was featured in a 1926 *Redbook* magazine article with a full-page photo. At the time of her 100th birthday, Dazee was recognized as the world's oldest active newswoman. This exuberant piano-playing woman was referred to as the "First Lady of Cheyenne Frontier Days," the world's largest outdoor rodeo celebration. It's a ten-day rodeo festival that has been attended by thousands of people since 1897. Dazee is responsible for many of the floats still seen in today's CFD parades. She would ride on a float, hammering away square dance songs on the piano as they traversed the parade route. The float also included dancing girls with a bar where a keg was always drained during the parade route.[6]

Dazee and her husband, Lieutenant Charles Bristol, were married at the turn of the century in 1900 and lived in a charming home on the 700 block of East Twentieth Street for the remainder of their lives. I was fortunate to be able to tour the house a decade ago. I was enthralled by the charm of the grand staircase, the pocket doors and the built-in china hutch. The carriage house still remains and functions as a three-car garage.

Despondent after his diagnosis with malaria, Charles took his own life in the den of their home. Dazee remained in the home but never entered the den again. She never remarried. Dazee attended a school of writing and advertising in Denver, Colorado, so she could support herself. She was associated with the Cheyenne newspapers for thirty-seven years.

Dazee Bristol portrait, featured in *Redbook* magazine. She was a renowned journalist and the "First Lady of Cheyenne Frontier Days." *Wyoming State Archives Collection.*

Dazee and Charles Bristol's home, 2020.

Dazee lived to the young age of 105, passing away in 1983. My sister was her nurse when she was in the hospital during her later days, and she got a real kick out of this feisty woman. Even at her age, she didn't take any guff. When Dazee celebrated her 100th birthday, a large party was held for her at the Hitching Post Inn with more than six hundred people in attendance. Wyoming's Governor Ed Hercshler declared it Dazee Bristol Day.[7]

The Bristol home has had continued sightings and activity over the decades, through various owners and remodels. The couple's apparitions have been seen; Charles's apparition is glimpsed walking across the den and front entryway, where cold spots are noticed. Pet cats sit and stare into the den; if they enter the den, they stop abruptly and then turn and run back out.

The house was listed for sale after Dazee died, but the realtor couldn't stand to be inside the house for long, saying she felt a pressure in her head and was uncomfortable. Residents hear knocking sounds, especially at night. Often it sounds like someone is at the door, but when they check no one is there. The cabinet doors open and close on their own accord, and the shower is heard running in the middle of the night; when they go into the bathroom, the shower stall is dry.

Ashley slipped into bed during a thunderstorm one night. The lights were off, and the house was dark when she heard something loud fall in the bathroom. She stayed in her cozy bed rather than address the sound, but then her cats began hissing. She dragged herself up and went into the bathroom, but nothing was found out of place.

One morning, Ashley got up and fed her cats and then went back to bed, grateful she had they day off. Her husband was out of town. At quarter after nine, she heard the back door open in the hall under her bedroom. The cats sat up and perked their ears, listening to footsteps walking down the hall, a jingling of keys and then more footsteps. Alert now, Ashley heard the basement door creak open and then shut. With a racing heart, she began searching her home, calling out, but no one answered back. Carrying a baseball bat and a flashlight, she searched the basement's dark depths. She was alone in the house with her cats.

New owners bought the house in 2006. A few days after moving in, they heard a booming sound and ran to their son's nursery. The child's gaze was fixated in the corner of the ceiling. They did not find anything broken or moved.

# TOM AND HATTIE DURBIN'S HOME

I have known Tammy, the owner of this quaint Victorian home on the 1100 block of East Twentieth Street, for more than twenty years. I used to work with her mother, who also volunteered for Visit Cheyenne. Tammy has lived in this home since 1999. I first heard the story from Valerie Martin, long-standing trolley driver and paranormal enthusiast. Val knew the previous owners as well.

The home was built in 1885 by Tom and Hattie Durbin. Tom and his brothers brought the sheep industry to Wyoming when cattle were dying off as a result of harsh winters and drought summers. The sheep withstood the weather conditions better than cattle. Many local ranchers followed suit. The Durbin brothers supplied Fort Russell with meat for the soldiers.[8]

Initially, the Durbins' home was a small cottage with three rooms and a porch, but they made seven renovations to their home over forty-five years. It's now a substantial two-story home. A two-room addition was placed behind the cottage, and three rooms were placed on top to create a second floor. The windows in the enclosed porch are repurposed from an old Cheyenne bank. The Cheyenne Historic Preservation Board bestowed this home with a historic restoration award in 1987.[9]

Durbin Home, 2020.

Like most antiquated homes, there are always projects to be done. Every time any substantial home repair is undertaken, the Durbins' presence is perceived to be overseeing the renovation. Sometimes their apparitions are clearly seen.

In 2015, Tammy said that she glimpses the ghostly couple a few times a year. She notices that the air gets cooler and her dog goes into a frenzy when they are visiting. Her boyfriend was napping when he heard his name being called. Lazily opening his eyes, he bolted awake as a figure moved in front of the doorway. He immediately called to Tammy, but she told him not to worry—the Durbins are part of the home and won't hurt him.

I contacted Tammy last year to see if she had any recent visits. She said only a few; as usual, she thought they were just checking on things. Tammy was sure that the Durbins' spirits had closed the basement door on her one night when she was downstairs because it never closes on its own. There wasn't anything mean about it—they just wanted her to know that they were with her. The dog started barking ferociously at the same time. She just welcomed them home. They only stop by when the weather is nice. I guess they are fair-weather ghosts.

There is a story about Mrs. Durbin in the history books that puts a smile on my face and reinforces the notion of how strong the women of the Wild West were. Along with the majority of men in the 1870s, Tom Durbin followed his gold fever; this took him to Deadwood, South Dakota. Hattie, with her baby in tow, took the Cheyenne-Deadwood stagecoach to meet up with her husband. There had been a raid and murder of the stagecoach driver the day before. Afraid of another raid, Hattie hid $10,000 inside of her baby's diapers. They were stopped, but the money was not discovered. They made it to Deadwood unscathed.[10]

## SHED NEW LIGHT: BAILEY HOUSE

Cheyenne was established in 1867, and by the 1880s, it had become the wealthiest city in the nation (per capita). The cattle industry was booming. Carey Avenue was known as "Millionaire Row," and Seventeenth Street was "Cattle Baron's Row"; both were lined with lovely homes. Most from that era on Carey Avenue are gone today, but Seventeenth Street is still adorned with desirable housing. Governor Nellie Tayloe Ross's home is on this street.[11]

In 2009, I met Betty, the charming owner of the attractive Bailey House, built in 1902 on Cattle Baron's Row on the corner of Seventeenth Street and Maxwell Avenue. It is listed in the National Register of Historic Places, as are many on Cattle Baron's Row.[12] Edd Bailey, a former president of Union Pacific Railroad, lived there for years. He began his UP career at the age of eighteen as a baggage handler, making thirty-eight cents per hour.[13]

Some years back, Betty and her husband remodeled the house, and during the remodel, the power went out a few times. No electrical problems could be found, and the power company had no issues or explanation for the outages.

Edd Bailey, former Union Pacific president's home, 2020.

The couple felt that someone unseen was there with them, especially in the bathroom. It got to the point that Betty would not take a bath if her husband wasn't home.

Sadly, Betty's husband passed away in the home in 2005. One night a few weeks after his passing, she awoke to a bright shimmering glow coming from the bathroom. She thought that she must have left the light on, but when she went to the room the light was off. His spirit shed new light on the situation.

## MAYOR HOLLIDAY'S HOUSE

Former Cheyenne mayor Cal Holliday was so popular that the city named the nearby park for him. The Holliday family lived in the beautiful brick bungalow house that was built in 1918 and sat just a few blocks from the park on Pebrican Avenue and Nineteenth Street.[14] The family remained there for nearly a century.

In 2009, the Mortons bought the home with the intention of updating and selling it. During the process, they became very fond of the home. The previous owners warned them that there was some unexplainable activity

Mayor Cal Holliday's home, 2020.

happening here. The Mortons didn't think too much about it at the time but would come to remember the warning.

After a long day's work and worn out from remodeling, they methodically turned off all the lights in the house. As they settled into their car, they noticed that the light in the upstairs bathroom was on, although they distinctly remembered turning it off. One of them ran back in and turned the light off again. When they returned a day later, the light was on.

They continued to have issues with this light turning on and off by itself. The light in a second-floor closet was consistently going on and off as well. An electrician was called in to check the wiring, but he found no problems. Maybe the spirit is afraid of the dark.

One afternoon, the doorbell rang—it had an odd sound, not its normal ringtone. When they went to the door, no one was there. They resumed their project, but once again the bell rang. Again there wasn't anyone at the door, but they did have a strong feeling that someone or something was there with them.

A plumber was hired to work in the attic on a bathroom vent pipe; he was focused on his task when he heard someone walk up behind him. Turning to acknowledge the person, he found no one near him. The plumber hustled downstairs, gathered himself and then went through the entire house, but no one was there. He returned to the attic and hurriedly finished his job. He very politely told the owners that he would not be returning to this home.

# EDWIN SMALLEY HOUSE

During a book signing in October 2019, I was pleased to visit with Ken, the homeowner of the beautiful historic Smalley home that we had featured in the Trolley Frightseeing Tours in past years. The ghost story here was originally brought to us by Cheyenne Paranormal Investigations.

One of Cheyenne, Wyoming's most infamous Wild West stories involves a man named Tom Horn. There have been several books written about Horn, and a movie, *Tom Horn*, was released in 1980. He was played by famous actor Steve McQueen. Steve McQueen and his girlfriend, actress Ali MacGraw, came to Cheyenne in 1978 on motorcycle when he was preparing for the role. They were married in Holliday Park during a visit in 1973.[15]

In 1902, cattle detective Tom Horn was arrested for murdering fourteen-year-old Willie Nickell. Edwin Smalley was the Laramie County sheriff during this time and is best known for arresting Tom Horn. The home I'm speaking of was Sheriff Smalley's house.

According to the Cheyenne City Directory of 1868, the Smalley family is significant in Cheyenne's history. Edwin's parents, Benjamin and Mary, were some of the first homesteaders to locate themselves in a parcel of land in Cheyenne, near Crow Creek in July 1867. They were the first couple to be married in the new settlement of the Wyoming Territory. A year later, on June 27, 1868, they became the proud parents of their firstborn, Edwin John Smalley, the first white male to be born in the newly established community.[16]

Years later, in 1910, Edwin and his wife, Edith, moved into the house on the corner of Twenty-Second Street and Seymour Avenue and lived here until his death in 1937. They had one son, Robert, who lived to the age of forty-eight.[17]

The current owner, Ken, moved into this historic house in 1988 and has taken great care to preserve its historic integrity. He and his family have had numerous encounters with a ghost they have fondly named "Amy"; appearing as a teenage girl around thirteen years old, she is thin with blonde hair and resembles Ken's own daughters. They mainly see Amy downstairs and on the second floor, moving back and forth in the hallway. One of Ken's daughters continually sees Amy moving past her open bedroom door. As

Sheriff Edwin Smalley's home, 2020.

many as thirty people have witnessed Amy's apparition over the years. Amy's reflection is often noticed in a window or glass door. The activity was much more prominent when his children were younger. Ken has never found the ghost to be threatening in any way. There is more activity when the house is in a festive mood, such as a Christmas party. Amy loves a party!

Ken shared some interesting news with me. After a bad hailstorm, he was having his roof replaced. The installer asked if he knew that there was a round window in the home's peak that had been covered over. This was great news to Ken, and he had the workers reveal the window. They also discovered a small room that been walled up in this upper attic space. They opened it up and found several dolls and toys in the secret room. I imagine these are Amy's toys.

Cheyenne Paranormal Investigations (CPI) investigated the home and heard many noises throughout the house but could not say that the sounds were necessarily abnormal. The investigators all reported feeling uncomfortable on the second-floor level but couldn't explain why exactly. The temperature downstairs jumped as high as ninety degrees from a seventy-degree normal reading, which couldn't be correlated with any other odd events. Ken reported that several unusual sounds have been heard on various nights, sounding like something was dropped on a table in another room.

## Whitaker Home

English immigrant Dugald Whitaker broke ground on his stately home in 1901, on the very day of his marriage to Elizabeth Shires. She was the daughter of Eliza Mason Smith, the first county librarian in the United States, in the thriving western town of Cheyenne. Dugald was a member of the Wyoming Stockgrowers Association for forty-two years, serving as president for four of them.

This Colonial-style home, white with green trim, is two and a half stories. It's a clapboard home that sits at the corner of Nineteenth Street and Pebrican Avenue, just a block from beautiful Holliday Park. It was built at the turn of the century and boasted many newfangled luxuries, including ten-foot-high ceilings, electricity, running water and heat, complete with a fireplace in the master bedroom. This home has been impeccably preserved and received an award from the Laramie County Preservation Board in 1996.

The Whitakers built a stable with sleeping quarters for the hired help and a separate carriage house. The large carriage house remains today. The Whitakers' carriage is part of the Cheyenne Frontier Days Old West

Whitaker Home on Nineteenth Street, 2020.

Museum's extensive carriage collection. The couple also owned a ranch north of Cheyenne on Horse Creek Road that still operates.

A small elevator was installed between the first and second floors in the 1920s because Dugald had a heart condition and the stairs were too cumbersome for him. Dugald died in 1936; his wife, Elizabeth, passed thirteen years later in 1949.[18]

The current homeowners have lived there since 1993 and have kept the property in top-notch condition. They say they have not experienced anything unusual but read an old newspaper article that claimed different. The journalist had interviewed previous residents and wrote that the sound of people walking overhead could be heard. The footsteps would stop when they reached the first-floor landing. A door on the third-floor attic bedroom slams shut of its own accord with no airflow near it. A former live-in maid passed away in this bedroom.

Naomi often played there when she was a child because her friend Kelli's grandmother lived there. The girls loved to ride the elevator up and down, and they generally played in the attic room. One day, Kelli had to use the restroom, and she left Naomi unattended...or so she thought. When Kelli returned, Naomi mentioned a girl she was playing with. Kelli was confused, as there was no other girl visiting. They encountered the unknown spirit child on many occasions thereafter.

# BILL DUBOIS'S HOME (816 EAST NINETEENTH)

*The height-challenged fortune teller who escaped from prison was a small medium at large.*
—*anonymous*

Standing beside the Whitaker home is another superb house that Hiram Bartlett had built in 1895. The current owner, Bill DuBois, has lived there for many years. I had the extreme pleasure of being invited over for a dinner party one evening several years ago. I truly enjoyed the company and the home tour.

Cheyenne loves Bill, its best-known historian. He was a respected history teacher for many years. Bill's grandfather and namesake William DuBois was a renowned architect who was responsible for many of Cheyenne's most notable commercial buildings, including the Historic Plains Hotel, the

DuBois Home by Holliday Park, 2020.

Wyoming Supreme Court Building and the outer wings of the Wyoming state capitol building that were added in 1915. No wonder Bill loves Cheyenne's history so much—his family is such a large piece of it.

The story of Bill's home was acquired by Valerie Martin, Cheyenne Street Railway tour guide of twenty-seven years and still counting.

Hiram Bartlett outlived his wife by many years and required the services of a live-in nurse his last five years. Upon his death, the nurse told his attorneys that Hiram had told her she could have the house. The attorneys didn't know anything about the promise and needed it in writing to award her the home. She went to see a clairvoyant, who told her she would find a signed will in the basement of the home. She did! She was granted the house.

# WHIPPLE HOUSE (300 EAST SEVENTEENTH)

There is spirit activity at the exquisite Victorian Whipple House, built in 1883 on the corner of East Seventeenth Street and House Avenue on Cattle Baron's Row. Prominent families have resided there over the past 137 years. It was one of the first homes in Cheyenne to have electric lighting and telephones and exceeds 6,600 square feet.[19]

In 1894, wealthy merchant Ithmar Whipple sold his elaborate home to the highly respected Territorial Supreme Court justice John Lacey, who was referred to as the "Father of the Wyoming State Bar Association." Later in the 1940s, this house was converted into a seedy gambling den. Since then, it was a fancy restaurant and an art gallery and is currently being used as a psychologist's office.

Justice Lacey's mother passed away in the home after being disabled for a long, miserable period of time. She took a nasty tumble and suffered greatly from that point forward. John did all he could to ease her pain.

The structure provided an exquisite space to display art when it was a gallery. I was disappointed when the gallery moved out. The gallery staff often felt a nurturing presence they believed to be that of Mrs. Lacey. The gallery was closed one weekend, and when they returned on Monday morning, they found various works of art laid out neatly on the floor. None of them had been in. They concurred that their spirit didn't like it when they were gone, as she likes activity and people around. Maybe she had some different ideas of where the art should be displayed.

A local resident wrote to me saying that the spirits acted out whenever the Whipple House was sold and renovations were done. In the case of one

Whipple Lacey House, 2020.

owner over fifteen years ago, she recalled that the work crews continually had weird things happen to hold up the renovation progress. The owners called someone in to do a cleansing ceremony, banishing the spirits. She said that the spirits then followed the family to their home instead of staying at the Whipple House. They showed themselves for several days before moving on.

The owners complained that they couldn't keep the lights on, as they were continually turning off on their own. During renovations, the owner kept a notepad by her bed. In the middle of the night, she sat up and drew a picture of a woman that she was seeing. It turned out to be a drawing of Mrs. Lacey.

## NAGLE WARREN MANSION

A former police officer spoke of a time when he had spent the night at the Nagle Warren Mansion. He heard a loud *slam* sound during the night, so he opened his room door and looked out into the hallway. Standing in the tower room was a woman in a long gown, about fifteen feet away. He clearly described her as having long dark hair and pale skin, wearing a dark-colored

Nagle Warren mansion, 2020.

dress with a light lacy layer over the upper portion, along with fluffy cuffs. She held something under her arm, but he wasn't sure what it was. He could see her but described her as being a bit out of focus. There was no negative feeling accompanying her apparition.

# Happy Little Visits

I received correspondence from a woman whose ancestors lived on the 2400 block of Warren Avenue for decades. The house has been leveled, replaced by a parking lot. Her ancestors George and Maria Clark came to Cheyenne in the 1880s and owned two small stores. They had lots of children; their son Clarence Clark served as the depot master during the 1920s, and he had been a conductor before that.

Clarence married Bertha, a fine woman. By the 1900 census, they had two living children and, sadly, two deceased children. The family story that has been passed down speaks of one girl dying at the age of four and another as an infant. The remaining family does not know the cause of the young girls' deaths, possibly scarlet fever. Bertha told her grandparents that she received happy little visits from the girls after they died and that they were happy up in heaven.

# Luke Voorhees Home

Luke Voorhees was among the first Cheyenne settlers before Wyoming was a state. He served as a territorial and county treasurer for four years and was also involved in the development of the Cheyenne Street Railway Trolleys. He was a veteran stagecoach operator who was placed in charge of the famous Cheyenne-Deadwood stagecoach after the owner was shot and killed during an ambush in 1876. Voorhees was justice of the peace at the time of his death in 1925.[20]

He built his gracious Italianate home in 1884, sparing no expense at 2110 Carey Avenue along "Millionaire Row," where the most successful businessmen lived. Fifty years later, the home was cut into two, and both sections were moved ten blocks. The owner at that time was Judge Riner, a member of the Wyoming Supreme Court for twenty-seven years. It remains

Both parts of Luke Voorhees's home. The house was split in two parts and moved ten blocks.

An original Deadwood stagecoach, driven by Luke Voorhees to the Deadwood, South Dakota gold rush. It is now part of the Cheyenne Frontier Days Old West Museum Collection.

two separate homes that sit beside each other; one faces Thomes Avenue and the other Twenty-Ninth Street. Most Cheyenne residents have no idea that they were once one home, each beautiful homes in their own right.[21]

The larger one was listed for sale a few years ago, and I was delighted to tour the home. It did not disappoint. It has exquisite stained glass, a perfect enclosed front porch and a gorgeous wide staircase with a banister that was made to slide down. I would not hesitate to live there, spirits and all.

One family did renovations and stirred up the energy in their home. While trying to sleep during and after the construction, they were kept awake by the sounds of unseen children laughing and playing in the night. The Voorheeses' obituaries don't list any children. There have been a few different homeowners since the Voorheeses lived here. Judge Riner and his wife, Mary, had three children, but all lived into adulthood.[22]

I met Casey, the dynamic granddaughter of the couple who had owned this house for more than twenty-five years. She is very close to her grandparents but had always refused to spend the night in their home, even when she was a little child. She always felt anxious in the house; the air felt thick to her. Casey described a huge unfinished basement that was "super creepy." When I toured the home, it didn't seem creepy to me, although I'm typically comfortable with spirits.

Casey said that while several overnight guests were in the home and everyone was tucked into bed, they were startled awake by intrusive sounds of banging pots and pans. They all converged in the kitchen but found no source of the noise. Banging pots and pans sounds like something children spirits might enjoy doing.

# DR. CROOK HOME

The gorgeous Victorian home at 314 East Twenty-First Street has quite a history. Built in 1885 for the beloved Dr. William Crook, the founder of the Wyoming Medical Association, it stands directly beside the Wyoming's Historic Governor's Mansion.

The house belonged to Josiah and Kate Van Orsdel; he was a Wyoming attorney general from 1898 to 1905, appointed by Theodore Roosevelt. Continuing in his political career, he was an associate justice of the Wyoming Supreme Court from 1905 to 1906 and a U.S. assistant attorney general for the Department of Justice from 1906 to 1907.[23]

Dr. Crooks's home on Twenty-First Street, located beside the Historic Governor's Mansion, 2020.

The home was owned by the Cook family, who operated a successful plumbing business from 1907 to 1955. Today, the house is the Wyoming Children's Society, founded in 1911. Orphan trains sent homeless children from the East Coast to West, helping to find families for orphans and assisting single mothers at a time when such situations were not socially accepted.[24]

Dr. Crook was Cheyenne's first permanent doctor and owned the city's first automobile, a 1903 one-cylinder Oldsmobile. Dr. Crook lost Ruby and George, two of his three children, within one week's time to scarlet fever in March 1880, prior to building this house.

In 1890, Crook leased the home to William Richards, who was then elected governor. For a brief time, this home served as the Territory of Wyoming's Governor's Mansion. Dr. Crook was the oldest practicing physician in Wyoming when he passed away in 1920 at age eighty-four from heart trouble.[25]

A large two-story carriage house adorns the backyard. The servants' quarters were built over the stalls. Adjacent to this is a small coal storage building. The chicken house has been remodeled into a covered patio.[26]

Years later, the home was converted into a rooming house, and residents grumbled that it was stuffy because the upstairs windows had been painted shut over the years. In the heat of the summer, they struggled to open the windows; even the strongest of the residents could not pry them apart. After many attempts, they gave up and went downstairs, only to return and find the windows had opened wide in their absence.

## BAXTER LOG HOUSE

Sitting on Morrie Avenue and Eighteenth Street to the west of Holliday Park is this odd-appearing L-shaped log cabin that looks out of place. Most people in the community haven't heard the interesting history of this cabin, which was built in 1885, twenty miles west of Cheyenne near the tiny town of Hillsdale, Wyoming. The 2010 census counted forty-seven people in Hillsdale. My daughter and her family recently moved there, so now there are at least fifty-one people living in Hillsdale.

The cabin belonged to the governor of the Wyoming territory, George Baxter, who served for thirty-eight days (November 11 to December 20, 1886) before President Cleveland reversed his appointment due to a disagreement over fences and branding.

Baxter Warren log cabin, 2020.

Francis Warren's family owned the log home from 1899 to 1961. Warren came to Cheyenne in 1868, when the untamed city was less than one year old. Warren was twenty-three, and he had just fifty cents to his name. Over time, he became involved in real estate, mercantile and livestock businesses as well as politics, becoming the wealthiest man in Wyoming. He went on to be Cheyenne's mayor and then later Wyoming's last territorial governor and the state of Wyoming's very first governor; then he served as a U.S. senator for thirty-seven years. Warren died in 1929 while still in office at the age of eighty-five, being the last Civil War veteran in Congress. In January 1930, President Herbert Hoover renamed Fort Russell to Fort Francis E. Warren, honoring the beloved public servant. It is now Warren Air Force Base.[27]

At the turn of the century in 1900, the Warrens took the log cabin apart log by log, numbered each log and hauled them into town by wagon. They reassembled the home like a jigsaw puzzle at its current location across from Holliday Park. It reminds me of Lincoln Log toys.[28]

In 2002, Valerie Martin learned about a ghost at the Historic Log Cabin. In Val's words, "It has something to do with dogs getting loose and killing the neighbor's chickens, and then the neighbors getting loose and killing the dogs!" She has a way with words, doesn't she?

The family frequently came home to find their pair of large dogs locked in the strangest places—once in the attic, with the door shut and bolted from the outside and once in the closet beneath the stairs, which was bolted from the outside. Especially strange, they found the large dogs tucked inside the kitchen cupboards on more than one occasion.

Angel, a member of Paranormal Hunters Observation Group (PHOG) who works with us on the trolley tours, was a previous tenant here. She lived in the main section of the home with her tween daughter. There were bullet holes inside the log cabin walls. The wooden floors and fireplace were still original, along with the creaking hinges and floorboards.

One day, Angel went to the dim basement to do laundry—her daughter refused to go down there because of her fear of spiders. Angel was astonished to find a lit cigarette. After extinguishing the cigarette, she looked around the basement; in a broken claw-foot tub, there was a really old pack of Winstons. Neither she nor her daughter had any idea where it came from. Angel and her daughter always sensed a male presence in the home and would often say, "Hi, Mr. Baxter" when they felt him around.

There was also an unusual painting left in the basement. Angel hung it over her bed. Her friends all had comments about the painting. Then Angel began having extreme nightmares. They persisted until she took the painting back down to the basement. For some reason, the spirit did not want that painting in the bedroom. Simple fix, fortunately.

# Antelope Inn on Warren Air Force Base

The Cheyenne Chamber of Commerce occasionally brings in professional speakers for events and membership drives. Maddie, from a Georgia company, was there in 2016, and she stopped in my office to share a story with me.

Several years ago, Maddie and her husband, Will, were stationed at Warren Air Force Base, so they were familiar with Cheyenne. When her company was brought on to speak at a chamber event, Maddie booked rooms at the Antelope Inn on the base since they still had military privileges. This included a neighboring room for her colleague Jennifer.

The first night they were here, Jennifer opened up a copy of my book *Haunted Warren Air Force Base*. Maddie discouraged her from reading it until after their stay at the base, but Jennifer was drawn in and continued reading. She became so frightened that she was too afraid to sleep in her hotel room alone and slept on the floor in Maddie and Will's room!

She did this for a few nights, and then Maddie sent her packing to her own room. That next morning, Maddie and Will awoke to find the drop ceiling tiles in their hotel room all slid over a few inches and not in their rails. This unnerved them. When they went to check on Jennifer, they found her fearfully staring at a big pile of sand on the floor of her room that had unexplainably appeared.

There is indeed a lot of spirit activity at Warren Air Force Base.

# Pershing House Restoration on Warren Air Force Base

Rick and his boss, Jim, were doing some restoration work on the older homes at Warren Air Force Base in November 2005. They were in the basement putting in a new window when Rick's "spidey senses" alerted him; he turned and saw a full apparition of a Union soldier, just standing there. The soldier appeared to be peeved that they were there in his house. Rick managed to get his boss's attention. When Jim looked over and saw the soldier apparition, he blurted out "We're done," hastily grabbed his tools and rushed out.

Another day, Rick was upstairs in the same house, once again replacing windows. He looked up and saw a beautiful woman from another era in the sitting room. He was truly taken by her. She had long dark hair and was in a full-length yellow gown. He stood there frozen, intoxicated by her beauty; he couldn't take his eyes off of her. She waved to him and then strolled through the house, looking at things while he remained spellbound. Once he snapped out of it, he hustled out to his car and sat there for a while…waiting for her to leave.

CHAPTER **9**

# TIMEKEEPER

*Lost time is never found again.*
*—Benjamin Franklin*

## TIME IS OF THE ESSENCE

Amy lives on East Seventeenth Street in the Rainsford Historical District. This is a neighborhood where wealthy cattle barons built their homes in the late 1800s. There are still about one hundred carriage houses remaining.

Amy's mother called her late one night saying that she could hear a weird humming sound in her living room. She couldn't detect what was making the noise, and it was driving her crazy. Amy could hear the loud noise through the telephone, so she headed straight to her mother's home a few blocks away to get to the bottom of it.

Her mom met her at the front door. The blaring sound seemed like it was coming from all directions. Amy walked around the living room, homing into different areas and trying to locate the source. She listened to the lamp and then put her ear to the electrical socket; she traced the sound up the wall to a clock. She grabbed the clock and swiftly turned around, exclaiming "*This*!" to her mother.

Her mom got the craziest look on her face and said that the clock hadn't worked for years, and now all of a sudden the alarm was going off. Amy set the clock back down on the shelf and realized that somehow it was set to the correct time. The women instantly lit up with goosebumps because they knew it was Grandma, who had recently passed over. What a way to get their attention and let them know she's still around. The experience left them with a sense of peace, knowing that Grandma was with them.

# TIME GOES ON

Ruth and Bernie used to live in a moderate brick bungalow home on Warren Avenue. Bernie collapsed and died by the lilac bush out front. Later, when Candice was living there, she told me of peculiar things happening in her home, such as the dogs staring at the television, even when it was turned off. Sometimes the remote control wouldn't change the channel, even with new batteries. Apparently, Ruth and Bernie liked the show that was playing. The lights would go on and off by themselves in the garage, which had been Bernie's domain.

Candice believed that Ruth's spirit locked one of her dogs in the bedroom. Another time, the walk-in closet door in the bedroom was locked from the inside. She could not figure out how that could have happened. Candice had to take the door off the hinges to get in.

Candice's mother gave her a grandfather clock in 1973. It had quit working two years before this, stopping at the exact moment Candice's mother died. It's been set at the same time ever since.

Future owners of the house came in to rent the trolley one day. When I learned their address, I asked if they had any unusual activity. They, too, have had the garage lights go on and off with no human assistance. Doors have slammed closed in the middle of the night when there were no windows open to cause an airflow. They have smelled cigar smoke and said that the previous resident told them he smelled it too.

# GLASS REFLECTION

Hal and Claire live on Leisure Street in Arp Addition, a housing development on the south end of Cheyenne. Both have seen spirits in their home.

Hal couldn't sleep and was wide awake doing dishes at three o'clock in the morning. Their five-year-old granddaughter was spending the night, so when Hal saw an image in the window peering at him, he thought it was his granddaughter's reflection. But when he turned around, no one was there. He checked on his granddaughter, and she was sleeping soundly. He admitted that he has seen the apparition of a small girl several times.

One day, Claire turned the corner into the hallway, where she abruptly stopped and put her hand up to guard herself. There was a form of cloudy mist right in front of her face. She watched as this vapor dissipated. She's not sure why, but she felt this was a male entity, as she realized it did not mean her harm.

Another spirit roams the Arp Addition. Hal tells of talk throughout the neighborhood of a lady spirit, a pioneer woman they call "Sarah." The story goes that Sarah was a prostitute who froze to death in this very rural area. When the weather turns from fall to winter, Sarah is said to go down the block, turning up the thermostat to ninety degrees in every house, causing arguments between husbands and wives!

# Acoustic Melody

Janice, who rode our ghost tours a few years back, also lives on Leisure Street near Hal and Claire. Janice also experiences activity in her home. Her family hears guitar playing in their home for hours on end, with the melody coming from the back bedroom, but nobody from this realm is in there. They've investigated everything they can think of but have found no tangible source. The neighbors also hear the music—hopefully it's to their liking!

## CHAPTER 10
# LOVE AND KISSES

*A kiss is a secret told to the mouth instead of the ear;*
*kisses are the messengers of love and tenderness.*
*—Ingrid Bergman*

## SEALED WITH A KISS

There is a quaint home on West First Avenue where the homeowners were continually finding bright-red lipstick lip prints throughout their house. Oddly, the lip prints would appear and disappear on their own. They couldn't make sense of this.

Later, a painter they hired asked if they knew the lady who had built the home and had lived there for years. They had not. The painter fondly recalled that she was quite a character. She had bright-red hair and always wore red lipstick. The owners now know that she remains in her home but is happy sharing the residence with them, as it is sealed with a kiss.

## KISS ON HER FOREHEAD

Jenny lives in a quaint flagstone house on the 1300 block of East Twenty-Third Street in the neighborhood north of Holliday Park. She hears footsteps going up her staircase many mornings around 5:30 a.m., but she lives alone.

This upset her at first. She has seen an apparition of an elderly weathered man on a few occasions. It's more of a silhouette; he is about five feet, nine inches tall. Jenny soon realized that he was not mean and rather was just part of the fabric of her house.

One night, she fell asleep on the couch. She woke up to a gentle kiss on her forehead and heard, "Good morning, granddaughter." Jenny doesn't believe this is her grandfather because he's not the apparition she has seen. She believes it's a former resident of the home, but it was such a sweet gesture that she doesn't mind the affection.

# A SIGN OF LOVE

I met Troy in 2014. His story warms my heart. His family moved to Cheyenne from Nebraska in 2011, purchasing a home on Andover Drive. Troy came ahead of the family to start his new job, and the family joined him later.

He felt uneasy in his new home at times. He did not feel like he was alone. Not wanting to concern his wife, he didn't mention it to her, but when she came for the weekend, she said she felt like someone was watching her.

The couple was doing renovations, replacing the kitchen flooring with hardwood and redoing the ceiling. Renovations often stir up energy that has been absorbed into a house for decades.

Tucker, their pet schnauzer, displayed a new behavior in this home, acting as though he was watching someone, turning his head from side to side. Often Tucker would cower, trembling and tunneling under the blankets. It happened so frequently that they took him to the vet to make sure he had no physical problems. The vet didn't have an answer for them.

The family came home from the store one day to find all the dresser drawers in their bedroom pulled open. There were no other signs of a break-in or theft. They didn't know what to think.

Their nineteen-year-old daughter called her mom saying that she could not get the bathroom door to open. She tugged, pushed and pulled to no avail. Giving up, she went downstairs to use that restroom, and when she returned to the upper level, the bathroom door stood wide open.

Troy's wife went to the library and learned that an elderly man named Bill had passed away in the home. This explained the handcrafted sign hanging on the flower garden fence: a heart with a cupid's arrow and an inscription reading, "Bill luvs Ada."

A bit more research revealed that Ada was in a local retirement home. They graciously returned the sign to her. The spirit activity stopped in the house after the sign was returned to his beloved Ada.

# PRIVACY LOCK

Around the corner from Bill and Ada's is a home on Milton Street that belonged to Blanche for decades. The current owners say that she is still around. Blanche starts the dishwasher and slides things off shelves—for instance, an air freshener went zooming across the room, apparently not her favorite scent. The toilet flushes when no one is in the bathroom. Oddly, that happens in many places with paranormal activity. Water is an energy conductor, so possibly flushing the toilet is one of the easier ways for the spirits to move energy.

There are occasions when Blanche won't allow them in through the back door. Generally, the door works just fine, but not when she wants her privacy. It can be unnerving when things fly around the room, but honestly, I think Blanche just wants to be acknowledged.

# TRAVELING GHOST

In 2019, I was doing a presentation for a group of retired state employees. The women at my lunch table were very interesting and told some great stories. I love giving presentations because it's generally followed up by people gathering around to share their personal accounts. I greedily soak them up.

Darci's family has a traveling ghost. Her father was in the military, and the family moved every few years when Darci was growing up; it seems the ghost tagged along with them. They fondly refer to her as "Gertie." I suggested that it was a family member, and Darci agreed, as she believes it is her great-grandmother.

Gertie is still hanging around at Darci's parents' home on Duff Avenue, which happens to be in the same neighborhood as the last two stories. But in this case, it's not about the house—it's about the family.

## CHAPTER 11
# FORGET ME NOTS

*Never forget me, because if I thought you would, I'd never leave.*
*—A.A. Milne*

## SAFETY FIRST

In 2018, I met Sheila, a lifetime resident of Pine Bluffs, Wyoming, a small town of under 1,200 people that sits at the Wyoming-Nebraska border. Sheila told me about her late husband, who had died when their son was just eighteen months old. A few years later, Sheila kept finding her son lying on the floor outside the bathroom door. She pondered why he would do this, recalling that they had a routine in the evenings when he was a baby. His father would give him a bath and lay him on a towel just outside the bathroom door, where Sheila would scoop him up and put his pajamas on. She realized that her son would have been too young to remember that occurring but thought maybe he saw or felt his father's energy in that spot.

Some years after her husband's death, she noticed a spark coming from a plug-in in their living room. An electrician came over and found charred wood and black soot from flames inside the wall. He said it was a miracle the house didn't burn down—he really couldn't explain why it didn't. Sheila believed her husband had been looking after them.

## SISTER TEA PARTY

A woman called into a Cheyenne radio station in October when they were discussing ghosts. She relayed the tragic story of the death of her two sisters before she was born. She never met them, at least not in a physical sense. When she was about four years old, she loved to play tea party. Her parents watched in amazement as she carried on conversations with invisible partygoers. She told them she was having tea with her sisters. This went on for more than a month. One day, her mother heard her crying in her room and asked what was wrong. She said her sisters wouldn't be staying for Thanksgiving, as they had to go back to heaven.

## A GRANDMOTHER'S LOVE

Andrea was on vacation in Hawaii while she was pregnant. One day, she smelled roses when there were none around. She had come to know that her grandmother's spirit was near when she smelled roses. That night, she lost the baby. It was devastating, but she was comforted to know that her grandmother was there with her and had been there for her child's spirit.

One month later, Andrea's father had a near-death experience. During the moments he was not breathing, he saw his mother holding the baby. He had a glimpse of eternity during his brush with death. Andrea was grateful for the validation that Grandma was caring for her child.

## GRANDMA ROCKS

Valerie Martin has been a devoted historical guide and driver for the Cheyenne Street Railway trolleys since 1993. In her primary job as a school bus driver, she spoke with another bus driver who relayed stories of his childhood. He said that all the grandkids spent a lot of time at their grandparents' little brick bungalow home on Reed Avenue close to Warren Air Force Base. They would play in the basement and were commonly in the company of an older, red-haired woman sitting in a rocking chair knitting. This was their deceased great-grandmother. They knew she wasn't alive but still felt comfortable in her presence.

# RAM'S HEAD

Tina was a trolley passenger on a tour given by Valerie Martin, and she shared her touching story. Tina's dad would teasingly turn the ram-shaped hood ornament on her truck sideways whenever he walked by.

One day, Tina's boyfriend had a strange feeling and recommended that Tina call her dad, as something felt wrong. She had talked to her dad earlier that day and so did not follow his suggestion. A short time later, Tina was heading off to work. In her driveway, she noticed that the ram was turned sideways. Then she got the call: her dad had just passed away unexpectedly.

Earlier in this book, I talked of intuition and listening to your gut. The feeling Tina's boyfriend experienced is a prime example of why. This is considered a clairsentient experience—when you just *know* something. I also knew when my husband passed away, as the anxiety took over. Then the police came. Always listen to your gut.

Through my entire pregnancy with my second child, I knew it was a boy. This is before the doctors would tell you the gender of the baby. I began decorating the baby's room in blue as soon as I learned I was pregnant. My family and friends kept saying I should do a more gender-neutral décor in case it was girl, but I wasn't worried. About six months along, I dreamed of a sweet little boy about two years old in the water on a floatie. I remember that dream vividly. The child in my dream looked exactly like my son did when he was two years old. Trust your gut.

# SPREAD ASHES

Helen had lived in her comfortable home on Granite Street for more than thirty years. She had never noticed anything disturbing in her home before her sister Carla's passing. Carla's remains were cremated, as requested, and the ashes were placed in an urn and put in a prominent place in

Helen's home. However, Carla had asked to have her remains spread in New Mexico, where their parents lived. Helen had good intentions of making the trip to New Mexico but procrastinated for some time.

Then it started. Every night, in the wee hours, both of Helen's bedroom lamps would simultaneously turn on. Wearily, she'd turn them off. As soon as she was resettled into bed, the lamps would turn back on. This continued night after night until Helen finally took her sister's ashes to New Mexico, fulfilling Carla's last wishes. The nightly interruptions ceased.

## CHAPTER 12
# STICKING AROUND

## HUGGING GHOST

In the Rainsford Historic District, just down from the Bailey House and the Captain's home on Cattle Baron's Row, we find another charming home. Pam rented the house on the east 500 block of Seventeenth Street and loved living there, even though she quickly knew that it came with more than one entity.

From outside, Pam would look up to the upper-floor window and often saw an empty rocking chair swaying on its own. Repeatedly, she would hear the front door open; she would count footsteps as they ascended each of the thirteen stairs and then listen to steps across the second floor above her. She also heard the porch door open on its own quite often. These spirits like to come and go and did this traditionally by going through the door.

There's a particular spot in the basement where she always smelled a sweet floral perfume that brought grandmotherly images to her mind. Her two-year-old son would often chatter about a lady in the house. This didn't concern her because she knew he was seeing an apparition that really existed and was gentle.

Standing at the kitchen sink, looking out the window, she frequently felt transparent arms reach around and lovingly embrace her. Intuitively, she knew it was the grandmotherly entity and freely received the blissful energy of her hugs.

Quaint home on Cattle Baron's Row.

A medium visited Pam and relayed that there were three or four spirits lingering there, which did not surprise Pam in the least. Had the home not been sold, Pam would have never left it. She noticed an energy change when she began to move her things out. Her new apartment was just around the corner, so she toted laundry baskets of her possessions to her new place. Since she always came right back for another load, she left the door unlocked, but when she returned the door was always locked. Good thing she had her key. Pam speculated that the spirit didn't want her son to leave, a feeling that was validated when big pieces of the ceiling in the boy's room crumbled down directly into his crib when they weren't home, displaying the spirit's displeasure over their departure.

## SKELETONS IN THE CLOSET

We often hear tell of folks with skeletons in their closet. I don't know that this closet has a skeleton, but it does have a spirit. Maxine, the resident bulldog at the home at the corner of Van Lennon and Twenty-Second Streets, was utterly obsessed with a living room closet. Animals have a keener sense than

## Home Is Where the Heart Is

Historic home at Twenty-Second Street and Van Lennon Avenue.

humans; they rely on their senses for survival. Dogs hear four times the distance that humans can. Maxine walked up to the closet and placed her nose firmly against the door; her owners couldn't coax her away. She'd sit there for hours on end. When they opened the door, she'd jump back a ways and then guard the area, staring intently into the closet, alerting her master to the presence within.

The owners loved the home but decided to retire and downsize, so they sold it. Before moving, they had a garage sale. A lady who came to the sale told them that her deceased husband had grown up in that home. They went inside, and the lady pointed to the closet in the dining room and said, "Grandma always said that closet is haunted."

There is another interesting fact about this home. There were two furnace ducts that had never worked. John called in a repairman in 2012. He found two dueling swords shoved into the heat duct! They are sharp fighting swords, not harmless practice swords. They had mauve leather straps wrapped around the handles. These swords were obviously hidden here; one must wonder the story and the motive behind hiding the weapons.

## SPIRITS AND LIBATIONS

A block farther east on Twenty-Second Street, they experience activity such as hearing footsteps when no one else is in the home and things being moved. Kelsey grew up in the home and is used to it, so she doesn't get a negative feeling, but rather a positive, comforting feeling when there, as a home should be.

Kelsey woke up during the middle of the night when she heard a racket of sounds coming through the vent in her bedroom. She sat up and listened; it sounded like a party, with varying voices and glasses clinking. Kelsey tentatively headed downstairs to the main floor, but it was dark, quiet and empty. Puzzled, she went down to the basement, but again, no one was there. Everyone was snug in their beds and sound asleep. A bit frightened and very bewildered, Kelsey sauntered back up to her bedroom. When she entered the room, she could still hear the festivities! Spirits and libations abound. They party chatter lasted about five more minutes, but she did not sleep the rest of the night.

## MAGIC LAMP

Here's a story my dear friend Rose told me. Her mother had passed away years ago, and she went to stay in her former home. Everything in her mom's room had remained the same over the years.

While thinking of her mother, Rose lovingly dusted and tidied up her dresser. A few days later, she noticed a small oil lamp on top of this dresser. She had not seen this lamp for forty-five years! Rose had given the lamp to her mother as a little girl and wondered what had become of it. She purchased the lamp with her own money, and her mother had commented that it was the sweetest gift anyone had ever gotten for her. She even gave Rose a big hug, something she was not prone to do.

Rose is certain that the lamp was not on the dresser when she dusted, nor in the home when they cleaned out the house after her parents passed away. She believes there was assistance from beyond this physical realm. My friend received a nod from her deceased mother.

# Fire Friend

An employee from Casper, Wyoming Parks and Recreation shared a remarkable ghost story with me after I did a presentation for her statewide convention group.

There is a house on Pheasant Street in the center of Casper where a young family lives. When their son Joshua was little, he had an imaginary friend, which they thought was cute. As time went on, they were surprised at how he kept including this imaginary friend in everything and was truly upset when they left the house, saying that he was sad because his friend couldn't go with them.

They questioned Joshua further about his friend because he was so consumed by him. Joshua said his friend was in a wheelchair and that he had burns from a fire. This was odd since the young boy hadn't been around any people in wheelchairs or any fire victims.

After a while, they decided to squelch their niggling curiosity and called the local fire department to see if they knew any history on their house. The fireman looked into it and called them back saying that there had been a tragic fire at that location many years ago and that a six-year-old boy who was wheelchair-bound couldn't get out of the house. He died in the fire, but apparently, he did not leave.

Children are much more receptive to spirits than adults because they have not yet learned that we are not supposed to believe they exist. As adults, we rationalize and shut down to the possibilities because they do not fit in the constructs with which we have been raised.

# Can You Hear Me?

There's a small, unassuming house located at Nineteenth Street and Dunn Avenue where a woman spirit slides the draperies back and forth and opens and shuts the drawers throughout the house. Most of the activity happened when a female friend would stop by to visit. This makes me wonder if this friend has some underlying psychic abilities and if the spirit was hoping to connect with her.

## UP ON THE ROOFTOP

Kent purchased a home on Lusk Lane in the Buffalo Ridge neighborhood. Many of these homes were constructed in the early 1970s. He became perturbed because most nights he would hear the clatter of footsteps on his roof, rudely disrupting his sleep. He would rush outside to catch the offender but would not find anything out of the ordinary.

On one occasion, Kent begrudgingly climbed up onto the roof, flashlight in hand, trying to find some indicator as to the cause of the noise, to no avail. He learned that a previous resident had a heart attack and died while working on the roof. The man had built a nice addition to the home. His craftsmanship was extraordinary, and it is thought that because he put his heart and soul into this project he has remained attached to the area.

## SWAMP MAN

A favorite stop on our trolley ghost tours over the years has been an attractive Victorian home on Warren Avenue situated across the street from the school administration building. The activity in the home has been ongoing for decades, and its story has evolved as we learn more.

Sisters Ellen and Stella grew up in the home, and seeing spirit forms was a common occurrence. One time, Ellen woke up to a face floating directly above hers. After that, she slept upstairs in a room with her older sister, Stella.

There was a safety gate with a latch at the top of the stairs on the second floor. Stella's bedroom was near the staircase. She would see a vivid figure that had "fringy things" hanging from its arms. She called this entity "the Swamp Man." It would open the gate, walk through, close the gate, enter Stella's bedroom and tickle her back. While it sounds scary, the actions seem playful.

Years later, Ellen and her husband, Matt, decided to purchase her childhood home when it came on the market, despite all the paranormal activity she experienced here as a child. The couple was excited to revive a piece of Cheyenne history. They completely gutted the house in a full renovation project. The construction workers became familiar with the entity in the home right away, as power tools began turning on or off by themselves. The radio would also turn on and off intermittently.

Occasionally, they would notice unusual aromas drifting through; in their words, the smells were similar to cherry pipe smoke and grape Kool-Aid.

# ROCK 'N' ROLL

A trolley passenger relayed that her neighbor had passed away in his home. Several years later, a young couple rented that home. They had a hard rock band and practiced in the basement. Sometimes when they would finish a set, it was followed up with loud stomping footsteps from above, but no one was up there.

The lady went on to say that the man who had died in the home was of strong religious beliefs, and she didn't think he cared for rock-and-roll music.

# ROLLING AROUND

There is a small home on Bradley Avenue with a lingering resident. An elderly couple had lived in the home. Following a paralyzing stroke, the husband was forced to live out his days in a wheelchair. After his death in the early 1960s, his widow rented the house to a younger couple. Whenever they went down to the basement, they could hear the sounds of a wheelchair rolling overhead.

# HOFMANN HOUSE

The 1890 Cheyenne home at Seymour Avenue and Nineteenth Street was neglected for the past decade. Now it has been given a facelift. The 1902 Cheyenne City Directory shows that this house belonged to Ed Hofmann. The Hofmann brothers were well known in town, owning a sizable saloon and gambling hall with the standard bordello of the day on Fifteenth Street, just down from the depot. There are stories about their saloon in the *Haunted Cheyenne* book.

Years later, another family moved into the home and lived there for many years to come. Caitlyn, age sixteen, was home alone, lying in bed and chatting on the phone, when suddenly the bed began to shake. Terrified, she immediately called her older brother, Joe, and begged him to come get her while she waited on the porch.

It was a crisp fall day. Joe's wife, Mary, waited in the car, while Joe ran in for a quick visit. He returned to the car with a perplexed expression on his face. His parents weren't home, but he could hear chattering voices inside that sounded like a large dinner party was happening. The voices abruptly stopped when he peered into the living room. Mary understood, as she'd often heard voices when she was in the house alone. The Hofmanns were prone to entertaining during their years in this home. Undoubtedly, the festivities continue. This is residual energy—events, happy or sad, replaying from the past and embedded into the home.

Lillie often found her cookie jar collection moved forward and sitting very precariously on the edge of the kitchen hutch. Each time, she pushed the cookie jars safely to the back of the hutch. They thought that the old floorboards might be starting to slant, but they checked, and the floor was level. Fleeting shadows and the family's deceased dog had been seen walking across the floor.

During a family gathering, they watched spellbound as a ladle briskly stirred to and fro by itself, then became airborne, flying up and out of the

Hofmann Home, 2020.

deep stockpot. The ladle forcefully hit a flashlight on the microwave above them and knocked it to the floor; the ladle landed in the middle of the room. This spirit wanted some attention. It's saying, "Yoo hoo, I'm here." A previous owner died in the home.

# PIANO

Lilly had an antique piano dating back to the 1800s. She often saw a gorgeous woman with long blond hair wearing a flowing red evening gown seated at the piano. Eventually, Lilly sold the piano but said nothing of the spirit woman to the new owner. Soon they called, saying they were seeing a woman in a red evening gown seated at the piano. I always appreciate stories where people who don't really know one another experience the same events associated with a place or object. It validates the experience.

# DON'T GO

The next story happened in a house that was built by the Union Pacific for employees on West Twenty-Fifth Street near Lakeview Cemetery. This house is adorned with a historic preservation award.

Frank the owner laughed and said that the ghost doesn't like the vacuum and shuts it off when they try to do the floors. Frank and his wife, Alexis, often feel that something is watching them in the home, especially when they were doing the final cleaning before moving out. Alexis was in the kitchen when she heard a loud *thump* upstairs, but she was the only person in the home. Frank returned and was repairing the stair railing when he heard growling right in his ear. He called out for Alexis. She told Frank that she could feel that the spirit was upset that they were moving. Normally, they felt no malice from the entity.

New renters moved in and reported that they experienced the ghost's antics. Their adult son came to visit them and see their new home. He informed his parents that he would never stay there again; he was totally freaked out by his encounters with the spirit, despite his parent's reassurances. Often spirits are just trying to get our attention, but that can be frightening to us humans.

Home on Twenty-Second Street, with an uninvited guest.

## UNINVITED ROOMMATE

While sleeping one night in his home in the east 200 block of Twenty-Second Street, Cliff was abruptly awakened; as his eyes focused in from sleep, he saw a tall, slender woman standing near his bed. She just stood there, curiously looking at him. He described her as pale with long straight black hair that flowed clear to her knees over her gray dress.

Another time, he felt her cozy up beside him. His eyes wide open, he glanced over. He did not see anyone but felt a cold hand rest on his chest.

One evening, Cliff and his roommate, Paul, were casually chatting when they heard a clanging noise. They glanced over to the source of the noise. A shirt on a hanger was hung over the top of the bedroom door. The men watched in astonishment as the wire hanger bent downward as though someone were forcefully pulling on the shirt. Suddenly, the hanger sprang across the room, and the shirt floated to the floor. No more wire hangers!

## WISPY GIRL

Tucked away, the quaint green house on East Twenty-First Street was built in 1938 and was the first house at this location. After buying it in 1994, Dillon didn't experience anything weird right away, but two years later, his girlfriend and her kids moved in. That's when the activity kicked up.

They often see a girl about twelve years old, with long hair, wearing a wispy white gown. The kids frequently see her in the basement playroom; many house guests have observed her as well. I believe she was happy to have the children move in, and that is why she made herself known to the residents. In the middle of the night, they sometimes see a green glow in the hallway. The wispy spirit moves things around and hides Dillon's cigarettes on top of a window frame. They notice more activity in the summer months.

## BASEMENT DWELLER

Mason's parents bought their house on Maxwell Avenue a block from the cemetery in the early '90s and still live there to this day. Mason admitted that he had an overactive imagination as a child, hearing noises and voices downstairs, especially after reading the *Scary Stories to Tell in the Dark* series.

When Mason was seven years old, his bedroom was moved to the basement. Every once in a while, he'd look over into the basement family room when he was going upstairs and would swear that someone was standing there. This caused him to run quickly up the rest of the stairs.

Fast-forward to about 2010. Mason is a married adult with two daughters. The family went to a parade and were getting ready to leave when his four-year-old daughter, Ivy, said she needed to use the restroom. Mason's parents' home was nearby, so they went there. Mason's mom was upstairs using the restroom at the time, so he took Ivy to the downstairs restroom. As they were walking up the stairs, Ivy started laughing. Mason asked her, "What's so funny?" She looked up at her dad and said, "That man, who is he?" while pointing to the living room. Mason picked her up and ran up the stairs.

Ivy's laughter makes me believe that this entity isn't bad. Mason just gets spooked by the unknown.

# TOM'S DO-NUTS

A very kind and well-liked man named Tom lived in a house on Nineteenth Street and Seymour Avenue for many years. He opened the first donut shop in Cheyenne; the bakery was in the basement, and he lived upstairs. There was a rear entrance that went directly into the basement, and customers would go on down to purchase donuts. Tom gave a free cookie to any child who stopped by in the morning on their way to school.

Years after Tom's passing, a young lady named Carol rented the home. It didn't take her long to realize that Tom was still around. Being a baker, Tom was observed in the kitchen rattling the hanging pots frequently. Carol's dog Baxter would sit in the kitchen doorway and stare intently at the hanging pots, cocking his head sideways.

When Carol and her friends were hanging out in the living room, they would hear a joyous laughter coming from the dining room. Carol's landlords had told her that the ghost of the previous owner was there but that he was friendly.

One night, Carol and her boyfriend were sound asleep when a noise awakened them and Baxter. They noticed a candle in a glass votive and a lighter on the floor in the hallway, quite a ways from the nightstand. The votive was shattered on the floor.

They assumed that this was the noise that woke them up, but they couldn't figure out how or why the candle and lighter fell off of the nightstand and had moved so far.

Carol had a friend visit who was very sensitive to the spirit world and immediately sensed Tom. Carol had not mentioned Tom prior to this. When they went downstairs, the friend overwhelmingly smelled cinnamon. Tom had kept his bakery spices in a pantry under the staircase, next to where they were standing. Carol now stored her gardening things in that closet, and it did not normally smell of cinnamon.

The friend was able to communicate with Tom. She said that Tom was pleased that Carol lived there, as he really liked her. Then he said that the candle flying off the nightstand was him warning them that someone was trying to break into the house. When the couple got up and turned on the light, it scared the burglar away. Her friend had not known about the incident before hearing about it from Tom on the other side.

# I'M OKAY

Amy was intuitive. She felt and heard paranormal things regularly, in all of the homes she had lived in. Bret, on the other hand, had not experienced anything paranormal until marrying Amy. Amy's close friend Stacey passed away, and the activity kicked up. The television would turn itself on, and the show *Law and Order*, Stacey's favorite, would always be playing. Bret began to notice knocking sounds. He was just dozing off when he heard a whisper, "Tell her I'm okay." He popped awake and noted that the air was extremely cold. He looked around, but Amy was sound asleep. Shaking it off, he lay back down. Again as he was drifting to sleep, he heard, "Tell her I'm okay." This happened a third time, so he finally told Amy.

# LITTLE NATIVE AMERICAN GIRL

Candace told us that she used to live in a house that was in the old Carlin Heights Division on the base; the area has since been torn down. That area is now called Peacekeeper, and the road is Minuteman Drive. She was at 5103A Minuteman Drive. Candace, her family and friends would see a sweet Native American girl. They could see her image in the mirror. She played with her children, and they would watch the toys move around. For thousands of years, Native Americans had the Wyoming land to themselves. The city is named after the Cheyenne Native American tribe. The word *Cheyenne* means "People of Strange Tongue."

# PARK PLACE

Some folks came into my office to talk ghosts one day. Their story goes back twenty years. Jason owned a home on Park Place Street. He lived in the upstairs level and rented the basement to his cousin Bret and his girlfriend, Anna. Bret and Anna mentioned that they constantly had electronics go off. The television would turn on in the middle of the night and scroll through the channels. The radio had a mind of its own. They unplugged it, but it still came on randomly and scrolled through the stations. There were no batteries in the radio.

The couple would hear footsteps upstairs when Jason wasn't home. The doorbell would ring, but no one was there. Sometimes Bret was standing right at the front door looking out, and the doorbell would ring when there was obviously no one there pushing the button.

# FORMER BROTHEL

We keep questionnaires on the trolleys during ghost tours. If people have had a personal paranormal experience, they can complete the form and share their story with us. In 2011, we received a completed questionnaire from Rachelle. She lives in a home on corner of Snyder and Thirty-First Street, which she said used to be a brothel.

Rachelle sees the apparition of a man out of the corner of her eye and also in reflections of mirrors and windows. She also sees a little boy spirit. Visiting friends have also seen the apparitions. She feels the spirit's presence but has not noticed any temperature changes. The scent of burning wood drifts through, and they hear footsteps. The lights turn on and off by themselves sometimes. She is comfortable living there, as it doesn't feel dark to her.

This home at Thirty-First Street and Snyder Avenue was once a brothel.

## RAILROADER HOUSE

There is a home on East Tenth Street south of downtown and the railroad tracks where spirits abound. The residents in this home frequently awake to the sounds of jumbled voices conversing in the basement—too many voices to understand. It sounds like a big card game, with gambling and arguing. Upon inspection, they find their basement normal and empty.

The family members often watch cups fly out of the cabinets and land on the floor, not broken, but standing perfectly upright. The saltshaker would slide across the stove or counter on its own. I questioned him about this being caused by passing trains. He said yes, sometimes when the trains went past they would feel it, but not at the same times these anomalies occurred.

## WHO'S THERE?

Jeff was renting an apartment in the corner home at Seventeenth Street and Evans Avenue around twenty years ago. He kept waking up in the middle of the night to pounding sounds on the walls. He couldn't make sense of where the sounds were coming from. Jeff complained to the landlord, who assured Jeff that the neighbors weren't doing it. Still, the pounding happened every night around three o'clock in the morning.

Home on Seventeenth Street, where a skeleton was found encased in the wall.

After a while, Jeff complained again; he wasn't getting any sleep. Finally, he convinced the landlord to check and see if animals were in the walls. They found a break in the wall. When they investigated further, opening up the wall, they found a body! The police were called, and they removed the body. Jeff moved out right away.

While this is a scary story on some levels, it's comforting that the spirit of a murder victim was able to find justice and peace. His disruptions resulted in his body being found. His body was laid to rest, so his soul could find peace.

# COMMUNICATIONS FROM THE AFTERWORLD

I saw these Cheyenne stories on Facebook about loved ones communicating with people from the other side.

Heather said that shortly after her dad passed away, the family struggled. She woke up one morning, and all the contents of the pantry were on the floor. She chuckled because she just knew it was her dad confirming that he was still around. Now, on occasion, they will find all of the TV components unplugged from the power strip that is under the entertainment center and very hard to access.

Another lady named Amanda said that her "Papa" was always a worry wart about everything, and her "Mammy" was the exact opposite. She always left the doors unlocked day and night, and he hated it. The day after he passed away, she woke up and all the doors were all locked.

After her Mammy died, Amanda's aunt was up at the house looking for a particular tie clip, but she couldn't find it anywhere. As her aunt was walking down the hall toward the door to leave, there it was: the tie clip was lying in the middle of the hall.

# PART III

# BUSINESS REPORT

*All the world's a stage, and all the men and women merely players:
they have their exits and their entrances; and one man in his time
plays many parts, his acts being seven ages.*
*—William Shakespeare*

CHAPTER 13

# TAVERNS AND CLUBS

## ALBANY BAR AND RESTAURANT

In Cheyenne's early days, Adolph Coors owned the corner of Fifteenth Street and Capitol Avenue, where the Albany Bar and Restaurant sit today. Adolph was the founder of the nationally successful Coors Brewery in Colorado. Coors operated the Depot Exchange Café, where he sold lunch and libations.[29]

The essence of the past lives on at the Albany. There are banging noises in a closed-off staircase going to the upper floor. Many of the staff members

Albany Bar and Restaurant.

refuse to go upstairs, where "shadow people" have been seen. They hear furniture sliding around the empty space.

There are two spirits regularly seen in the Albany Bar and Restaurant. One might be the victim William Ashford, who was shot there in 1892 during a drunken encounter; the other is an American Indian man that sits at the end of the bar. At least you'll never have to drink alone!

# DT LIQUORS

There are spirit encounters at DT Liquors on east Lincolnway Street, both in the libation form and as ethereal spirits. Employees have experienced oddities such as lights going on and off by themselves and wine bottles shooting off the shelves three feet above the floor. Astonishingly, the bottles never break; they just come to rest on the floor. The spirit is helping them to select the perfect beverage for the occasion.

# DANIELSMARK

Here's a little history on the charming house where Danielsmark's Brewery is located downtown on East Eighteenth Street. Samuel Corson moved to Cheyenne in 1883 and had George Rainsford design his whimsical cottage. It sits in the Rainsford District, named after this architect, who was recognized for all of the various roof styles in his designs. Corson became a prominent member of the community, serving in the Wyoming House of Representatives. Three generations of Corsons lived there.[30] Today, the popular Danielsmark's Brewery operates from the Corson cottage. The carriage house in the backyard is its brew room. Customers can enjoy brews inside the cottage or relax on the back patio.

This was Jim's daycare when he was young. He said that all the daycare kids played with an invisible little boy. The boy was blond and small. Adults couldn't see him.

I found Samuel Corson's obituary, which noted that his daughter, Mary, was just six years old when she died while living there in 1895. Samuel had no sons. Possibly it was a girl spirit and not really a boy, or it could be the spirit of a boy that lived there at a later time.

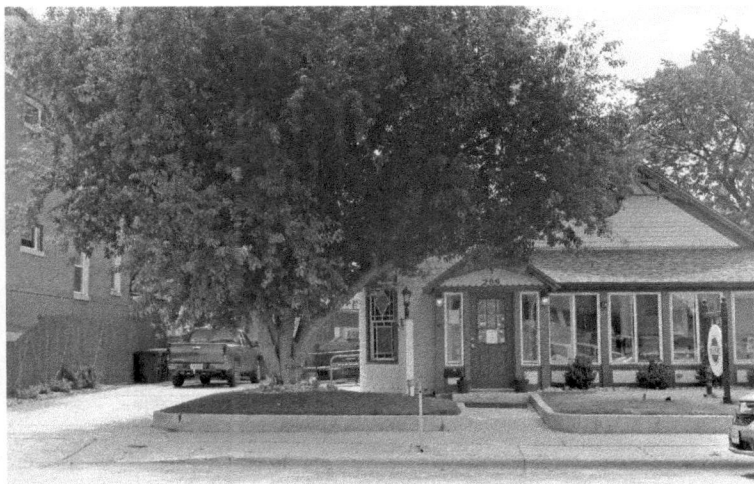

Danielmark Brewery in the historic Samuel Corson House on Eighteenth Street.

## CHEYENNE EAGLES LODGE

The motto for the Eagles Lodge is "People Helping People." Both of the known deaths that occurred in the Cheyenne Eagles Lodge at Lincolnway and Thomes Avenues were of natural causes. Originally, there was a German Men's Club at this location, but it burned down.[31]

Spirits remain in the Eagles Lodge. A shadowy figure is seen walking in the main hallway. He is not threatening, nor does he elicit a bad feeling. Some of the lodge members have felt a whispered breath in their ear and their shoulders being touched by invisible forces. A spirit is sensed in the bartenders' restroom; a few people have had the insight that his name is Henry, and one of them hears the song lyrics "Henry the 8th, I am, I am" whenever she is in the room.

Members have seen and heard a woman in a white dress who descends into the bar area. She is also experienced in the kitchen, as she often changes the water pressure and temperature of the water from the faucet, provoking the cook.

The basement contains billiard tables that are more than one hundred years old, along with vintage abacus scorekeepers. Some folks feel unnerved

Cheyenne Eagles Lodge.

in the basement, where strange noises are occasionally heard. The crawl space door opens on its own frequently. These spirits are members for life—and then some.

## CHEYENNE ELKS LODGE NO. 660

The Elks Club in Cheyenne has been at the same location at the northeast Seventeenth Street and Central Avenue since it was constructed in 1903. It was designed by William DuBois, who was mentioned earlier in this book. The lodge was one in a line of early fraternal clubs established along the transcontinental railroad. The basement originally had a billiard hall and cloakrooms; the second floor had recreation and lodge rooms. The grand meeting hall is on the third floor.[32]

Today's members sometimes experience unusual occurrences. A member said that they continually experience ghosts; chairs, glasses and other things being moved; unexplained noises and more. Some of the bar staff refuse to be there alone. Kerry said that her buddies went outside to smoke a cigarette, while she remained seated at the bar by herself—or so she thought. A tremendous noise then came from directly behind her. She sprang up from her chair but found no one there—and no cause for the alarming noise either.

Cheyenne Elks Club 1910 postcard.

## CHEYENNE MASONIC TEMPLE

The second Cheyenne Masonic Temple was built in 1901 on Capitol Avenue. After just two years, the building caught fire, as did many in Cheyenne's early days. The interior was gutted by the fire, but they were able to keep the original walls.[33]

Kris's niece is a member of Job's Daughters, a masonic group for young women, and his uncle is a member of the Masons, so Kris hung out at the Masonic Temple a lot as a kid. As kids, they were mesmerized by the frequent apparition of a distinguished man in a top hat, obviously from another time and dimension.

Glowing orbs are also common in the temple, as there are many photos and videos with numerous orbs taken from inside the temple. When Kris was seven years old, he wandered into a room, and the door slammed behind him. There was no draft or airflow, so he didn't understand why it closed, and it was really dark in there. He fumbled for the doorknob to get out.

Kris relayed that they could hear people playing basketball in the gym, the sounds of tennis shoes squeaking on the floor and a ball bouncing when no one was on the court or anywhere near it.

Cheyenne Masonic Temple. *Wikimedia Commons.*

Ruby has seen ghosts in the Masonic Temple several times. There is a lady spirit on the main floor, as well as a man on the second floor wearing a top hat standing on the balcony.

The Freemasons are members of a fraternal society that professes principles of "Brotherly Love, Relief and Truth." While women cannot join regular lodges, there are many female orders associated with regular Freemasonry, such as the Order of the Eastern Star. Paranormal Hunting Observation Group (PHOG) has experienced a lot of activity in the Masonic Lodge, and investigators have captured recordings of spirits conversing with them. They have audio of a spirit clearly indicating that he wanted the women to leave. Women are not typically in that part of the lodge, as it is a fraternal group.

When the temple was built a century ago, it included a barbershop that operated until the 1920s. Local barber Glen Chavez is a Mason, and members asked him if he would revive the barbershop business at the Temple, which he did in 2009. His shop is located on the second floor of the building. On opening day, a reporter from the *Wyoming Tribune Eagle* did a story on the barbershop, also taking photographs for the article. Once the film was developed, he realized that he had captured an image of a Victorian woman in a red dress, appearing in a mirror reflection. There had not been women anywhere in the area at the time of the interview.[34]

Kris is a member of the Freemasons and recounted that one windy evening, after a normal meeting, two other Masons and Kris were having a conversation in the main entryway. The front door opened and closed by itself a few times. He didn't think much of it due to the wind, but then he noticed that the door would open and close when there was no gust of wind at all; it was a rapid open-and-shut movement that's not really like when the wind pressure opens the door and then it slowly shuts. So, he went into the alcove and stood outside, waited and watched. To his surprise, he watched the door open and close with no accompanying gust of wind.

During PHOG's second investigation, the investigators spent some time in the gym and took a number of pictures using the infrared mode. After the investigation, they were shocked to discover two men on the upper level of the gym, one facing them and another facing left in the photos. Both had fedoras and 1920s-style clothing. While it's easy to often "see" faces or silhouettes in infrared pictures this image had sharp outlines of both entities.

Footage from another investigation showed a flashing light in a room at the end of the hall on the second floor. They described it as a faint, slow, throbbing glow. It was not the rapid on/off of a light switch being flipped. The team took many steps to debunk the light but could not shed light on the phenomena.

CHAPTER 14

# DINING

## ORIGINAL NAGLE HOUSE

Standing beside the elaborate Nagle Warren Mansion is the first home that wealthy merchant Erasmus Nagle built on the East 200 block of Seventeenth Street. This was the very first brick home in Cheyenne. Several restaurants have operated from this house over the decades with assistance from spirits.[35]

While Lucky Louie's Restaurant was there, a construction worker went upstairs to resume a project. He found his tools scattered around in a mess. He wasn't sure how they'd become so messed up, since he was the only one working. He neatly arranged the tools. He left briefly and returned twenty minutes later to find the tools in disarray again.

The waitstaff's trays have been knocked right out of their hands by an invisible force. Chairs are pulled out without human assistance, and the lights turn on by themselves at night.

When this was Lexis Restaurant, a waitress noticed two children talking to an elderly woman in Victorian clothing. Intrigued, she watched her descend the staircase. Wondering where this lady had come from, the waitress went downstairs to inquire. At the bottom of the stairs, she found a handful of staff members talking. The waitress asked them where the woman had gone and was met with blank looks. She understood this was the spirit of a woman who had lived here in days gone by. The waitress left flowers for the spirit on the stairs each month thereafter.

A 2020 image of the first brick home in Cheyenne, Wyoming, built by Erasmus Nagle.

Visions of an old cowboy of the 1800s have been witnessed by several people. He rearranges silverware and napkins. While remodeling the home into a restaurant, workmen arrived to find the front door locked. They knocked on the door and could clearly see a man inside, but he ignored them. Later, the owner came, and they asked why the guy inside wouldn't open the door for them. The owner said no one was there. Once they described the cowboy they had clearly seen standing inside, gazing into the fireplace, the new owner realized that this was the ghost he had heard about.

A customer who was dining alone was stunned when an old cowboy came and sat down at his table but refused to speak to him. Frustrated, the customer got up and found the manager. When the two of them turned toward his table, the old cowboy had vanished.

## Little Philly's

The staff at Little Philly's restaurant see a man dressed in 1800s-style clothing walking through the fast-food restaurant and looking at them. They have seen him several times, but he's never ordered anything. A former employee said that the staff calls him "Clyde." To let them know he's there, he slides things across the tables. He does this mainly in the evening when they are closing up the restaurant.

# BREAD BASKET BAKERY

The Bread Basket Bakery building was built in 1920; it became the Barnard and Stoll Grocery and Market in 1927 and lasted for forty-five years, until 1971. The store is on the corner of Nineteenth Street and Maxwell Avenue.

Mr. Werner Stoll, one of the grocery store partners, remained single his entire life and lived in a small apartment above the store. He passed away three years after the store closed. He never left.

I spoke to the ladies who work in the bakery and learned that on many occasions, a piece of equipment won't work. They become frustrated because they'll need to have it repaired, but when they return the next day, the equipment works just fine. They accredit the repairs to Mr. Stoll. They feel his presence and have heard him say hello. They have come into work early in the morning to find a loaf of bread set out and half eaten and believe that Mr. Stoll was making his presence known.

Bread Basket Bakery in 2020, formerly the Barnard and Stoll Grocery and Market.

## CHAPTER 15

# STOP, DROP AND ROLL

## OLD FIREHOUSE SPIRITS

There is an old firehouse on Eighteenth Street and Albany Avenue. It also served as the City Code Enforcement Office until the new Security Building was constructed downtown. Recently, it was converted into a family home.

Maddie worked there and had many paranormal experiences. They would often hear random voices inside the structure. The coffee mugs would disappear, and then they would find them days later in really odd places where people would not normally set them down. A locker would open and

This single residence home was once a neighborhood firehouse.

close of its own accord. While working, she would sometimes see a dark shadow figure bend around the wall and look at her.

On one occasion, three different witnesses heard disembodied voices talking at the same time, but they couldn't make out the words. They sometimes heard tapping, but there isn't a radiator or any known source for the sounds. One time, Maddie said out loud, "If this is someone that can understand me do the 'shave and a haircut, 2 bits' song," and then she heard, "Da da da *da* da…da da" tapped out in the rhythm of the tune. She blurted out, "We have to leave now" as she rushed to the door.

## ALL STOKED UP

Firefighters at the Dell Range firehouse sometimes have difficulty sleeping because they feel as though someone is pushing on their chests. Many feel that this is the spirit of a deceased fireman. They have had their beds shaken, and one had the blankets pulled over top of him. The ghost is hazing them as initiation to the firehouse. This spirit is helpful when there is a fire, as he says, "You got a call" before the call actually comes across the radio. This wakes the men, giving them a jump on the situation. Every second counts when the heat is on.

## CHEYENNE FRONTIER DAYS OLD WEST MUSEUM

The Cheyenne Frontier Days Old West Museum is a hot spot for paranormal activity, which makes sense because the museum is filled with old western relics and antique carriages. Objects can hold residual energy imprints, both negative and positive. I reported some of the museum's paranormal activity in *Haunted Cheyenne*, but here is new material.

The people at the Old West Museum have come to believe that there is a spirit attached to the old fire truck parked inside of the museum, as they experience it regularly. A manager came in one morning to discover a rope hanging from the ceiling above the fire truck. There has always been a lot of activity associated with this fire truck, and the staff began calling the spirit "Steve."

## BUSINESS REPORT

In October 2017, Paranormal Hunters Observation Group members were doing an investigation at the museum. Jose and Casey were standing beside the fire truck while a staff member was explaining the perilous hubcaps on the old fire truck that are referred to as "widow makers" because they are so difficult and dangerous to change out. Jose felt a robust tug on the back of shirt, and then he felt the shirt lift up. He thought Casey was messing with him; turning to chastise her, he saw that she had both her hands wrapped around the video camera and was taping the area. He asked her if she had pulled his shirt up, and she adamantly denied it. During a Halloween event at the museum, a medium who was part of the PHOG group told the museum staff that the ghost did not like being called Steve—his name is Jim.

There is a safety fire wall in the middle section of the museum that is supposed to automatically close when the smoke detectors go off to contain the fire so it doesn't spread. It goes across the whole width of the large room, sealing the fire in. This wall was not working, and they had called in several people to repair it, to no avail.

Mike and Ron decided to take a crack at it themselves. They completely removed the electrical box and disconnected it from the door. When it was time to go home for the day, they set the box aside and figured they would face the project the following morning. When they arrived the next day, they were astounded to see that the fire wall had closed. It was not even hooked up to electricity, so how in the world had this tall, heavy wall closed?

CHAPTER 16

# RISKY BUSINESS

## UNDERTAKER (GRIER'S BUILDING)

The large commercial building at the corner of Central Avenue and Lincolnway was erected in 1911 and held a furniture store for nearly one hundred years. A century ago, it was common practice to perform burial preparation in the same building where the furniture and caskets were sold.

In keeping with the times, merchants Hobbs, Huckfeldt and Finkbiner combined furniture and funeral services in this building. Bodies of the deceased were brought into the building through an entrance that still remains on the southeast corner of the store. After raising up the large door, a horse-drawn hearse would back down a declining ramp into the basement of the building. The bodies were moved from this unloading ramp to a small preparation room in the southwest corner of the basement. Caskets were displayed on the top floor, and funeral services were held in a small yet elegant chapel on the main floor.[36]

In 1948, after Mr. Huckfeldt and Mr. Finkbiner resided in caskets themselves, the sole survivor of the trio, Mr. Hobbs, sold the building to R.S. Grier, who continued operating a very successful furniture business there. Mr. Ed Georges, the most recent Grier's Furniture owner, worked many late nights in the building but had no ghost stories to share, even though it seemed to be the perfect setting. He took me on a tour of the building, and I saw the embalming room firsthand.

Former Grier's Furniture Building. Today, it is the Array School.

The temporary employees hired for the store's closeout sale were filled with apprehension when they were required to enter the basement after hours. An eerie feeling enveloped them as they descended the stairs. At the close of each business day, they would straighten up each level of the store, but in the mornings, they would find pillows scattered throughout the basement, where bodies were once prepared for burial.

## WYOMING BUSINESS COUNCIL

The Wyoming Business Council is just around the corner from the Albany Bar and Restaurant, facing Fifteenth Street and across from the Cheyenne Historic Depot. In the late 1800s, the west side of the council building was the Rex Hotel, while the east side was the Becker Hotel, the side with more supernatural activity.[37]

I asked Karen, who has worked for the business council for many years, if I could tour the building. She was kind enough to oblige and share their stories. There have been many sightings of a young boy's apparition at the business council. Young boy spirits are also sighted across the alley at the Atlas Theatre Building and the Wrangler Western Store. Two brothers, ages four and six, were killed at the Atlas location

Becker Hotel, now the Wyoming Business Council.

when two buildings collapsed in 1879. It's likely the same spirit in all three buildings. Brick-and-mortar walls are not boundaries for the dead.

There have been occasions when the business council staff would come in to work and find the small attic door opened; you need a ladder to access this door. They hear what sounds like a ball or something rolling back and forth above their heads in the tight attic, presumably by the young boy spirit. The sound goes both front to back and side to side. Sometimes they can hear this clear down on the first floor. This attic is filled with heating and air conditioning equipment, preventing a person from walking around.

Cassidy was there alone one weekend. The light in the copy room turned on by itself twice in an hour. She turned it off both times, only to have it switch back on, at which time she decided to leave. This could be the young boy spirit being a bit mischievous and having fun teasing Cassidy.

## MAJESTIC BUILDING

Before the age of the automobile, livery stables for boarding horses were located in every town—basically a parking garage for horses and carriages. In 1867, the Abney Livery Stable was built on the northeast corner of the Lincolnway and Capitol Avenue intersection. The horses for the original Cheyenne Street Railway trolley lived there.[38]

In 1907, the distinguished Majestic Building was constructed in its place. My favorite part of this building today is the vintage elevator, which requires a person to operate it. Several people working in the Majestic have reported unusual happenings, including hearing faraway indecipherable conversations throughout the imposing building when no one else is present. Venturing closer, the low static voices fade away.

In 2015, a businessman named Alex stopped into my depot office. He gazed out the window, looking across the plaza to the Majestic Building.

Majestic Building in downtown Cheyenne; originally, it was the First National Bank. *From* History of Wyoming, *vol. 1, edited by I.S. Bartlett, 1918.*

Under his breath, he made a comment about the building being haunted. When I inquired about his remark, he relayed that his good friend Travis had set up an art studio on the fourth floor. Travis began telling Alex that the building was haunted. Alex teased his friend, as he thought the notion was ridiculous.

Alex went to the studio one day when the building was devoid of people. The two of them were going down the empty staircase when they began to hear a couple of women's voices chatting directly in front of them. The men stopped dead in their tracks. They looked all around but saw no one. They bolted down the remaining three flights of stairs.

We received a similar account in 2007 from a lady who worked there. She said that there were many unusual happenings, and she often heard indecipherable conversations float throughout the building when no one else was present.

# WYOMING MEDICAL SOCIETY

This is the corner where the infamous Cheyenne Social Club once stood. The exclusive club is where the richest of the rich cattle barons

The corner building houses the Wyoming Medical Society Office. The infamous Cheyenne Social Club was once located at this site. Unfortunately, it was razed in 1936.

spent their spare time. One of the employees at the Wyoming Medical Society, located there today, relayed that out of the blue the water would start running from the faucet or the toilet would flush when she was the only employee there. I hope the gentlemen ghosts put the toilet seat down for her.

# DEPOT

There is a chapter about the Cheyenne Depot in my first book, *Haunted Cheyenne*. The building is continually giving me new material.

One evening, there was a wedding reception in the Cheyenne Depot's main floor lobby. Lynn was on duty. She went upstairs for a bit of solitude. While she was in the depot museum on the second floor, she saw the big double doors open and shut...open and shut...open and shut—three times consecutively, with no human assistance. She high-tailed it back downstairs.

Phil was upstairs in the Depot Museum, where they exhibit an intricate model train set, complete with miniature buildings and scenery. Phil walked out of the train room into the hallway, heading toward the steps, when he saw a man and greeted him. The man did not respond. Shrugging off the rudeness, Phil began to descend the stairs; he noticed that the man was directly behind him on the steps. When Phil reached the main floor landing, he turned, but the man was gone. He looked all around, but the man had vanished.

In my opinion, the man did not respond because this was residual energy. Phil was seeing the replay of the man from many years ago. A workman has been sighted throughout the building many times over the decades.

When a new employee starts at the depot, we all wonder how long it will be before they have their ghost initiation. Amber was there only a few weeks when she walked out of her office one day; she went to close the door behind her, but she felt a strong resistance. Odd, she thought, and pushed harder against the door. She couldn't close it, as there was an unknown and unseen force pushing back. This door is normally easy to open and close. A few minutes later, she was standing behind the museum gift shop counter when she saw and physically felt something wisp right past her. This has happened to previous staff as well. One of the depot janitors said that he hears the printer go off in the depot visitor center at 11:00 p.m. when no one is there.

Cheyenne Historic Depot main staircase.

A local pastor was perplexed when he was alone in the main floor men's room and heard a loud sigh as if a person were standing right beside him, but he was the only visible person in the room. When he exited the depot, his wife pulled up in her car. He bent down and was giving her an account of what just happened. When they were done talking, she pressed the automatic window button to close the window, but the glass did not slide up. She tried several times to no avail. After she pulled away from the depot, the window closed with no problem, and she has not had any issues with the window before or since that time.

Late one evening, a local businessman was descending the historic depot's original staircase. When he reached the main floor landing, he was overcome by the sensation that someone was behind him. Nervously, he turned his head and looked over his shoulder; there was an apparition of a man floating in the stairwell a flight above him. Frozen in his tracks, he stood there searching for a reasonable explanation when the specter vanished.

Delmer works in the depot building. He came into my office one morning to tell me that he had heard the voices of two women speaking from the historic stairwell, but when he checked, no one was there.

Another evening, a businessman was in the men's room. He was surprised when he heard someone moving in the next stall because he thought he and Stan were the only people left in the building. When he exited his stall, he noticed that there were no feet in the next stall over, making him uneasy. He quickly washed his hands and then heard two loud pounding sounds like someone hitting the stall door. He dashed out.

We have had numerous encounters in the depot with a child spirit that truly enjoys teasing the staff. This child is heard giggling and running in the hallways. Scarlett was trying to wrap up a big project and was still at work at 10:30 p.m. one night in March. The janitor had finished up and said his goodnight. Engrossed in her project, Scarlett jumped out of her skin when she heard the child laughing uncontrollably. The chuckling was coming from directly in front of her desk, just a few feet from her face. Scarlett was so flustered that she jumped up and walked in circles in her office, trying to comprehend what was happening. The laughter ceased, and she heard the distinctive sound of the push-bar door click open and thump close. She called out, "Who's there?" but Scarlett could not see anyone. Heart racing, she grabbed her purse and left.

Moving forward a few months, it was midday and everyone in the office was either at lunch or heading to a meeting, except for Scarlett. All of a sudden, a slamming sound resonated from across the hall, shaking Scarlett out of her thoughts. Cautiously, she arose and crept into the next office. Her co-worker Amelia had a shelf in the corner of her office. The top shelf had several picture frames displayed on it. A photo of her co-worker's son was sitting facedown; this is what she heard slam down, yet the remaining frames had all been rearranged on the shelf. As before, she heard that push-bar door click open. This door is not accessible to the general public but goes into a storage space. "Hello," she timidly called out, tentatively walking toward the door. No one was there. "Not again," Scarlett thought. Just then, three chairs on her right tipped over simultaneously. She completely lost her composure and came to get me where I work in the next office over.

Another morning, Lynn and her kids had gotten off the elevator on the second floor. Most of the kids were in the bathroom. Lynn walked out of the restroom, where her five-year-old daughter was standing near the elevator.

Her daughter said, "Mommy, who's that girl?"

"What girl?" Lynn asked.

"Look, she's down the hall by the Chamber Office." Her daughter replied. Lynn looked and didn't see her. Her daughter nonchalantly said, "She left. She was like my age, and she had on a long white dress. I've seen her before—remember, I told you."

As documented in the *Haunted Cheyenne* book, this child has been heard in the depot lobby by various people.

During Cheyenne Frontier Days, the depot janitorial staff has their work cut out for them. The depot is a downtown hub and is filled with vendors and activity during the ten-day festival. Cheyenne is bursting at the seams at the end of July each year.

The crew were wearily cleaning the third-floor offices when Dawn screamed. Scott came running to her aid. Dawn was pointing into the depot management office, stammering that there was a man. Scott followed her gaze, and he could also see him. The man was from another era, wearing a suit and a bowler hat. They were able to distinguish his features, even though he was a bit translucent. After a moment, the apparition faded away.

Once they calmed down, they continued their chores, knowing that everything had to be ready for the next day's events. They were cleaning the door window glass of the chamber of commerce office on the second floor. Dawn was standing inside the office, and Scott was outside in the hall, each spraying and wiping their side of the glass. Just when they had completed their task, they were stunned to see sets of fingerprints walking up the window, marking their clean glass. The activity continued through their shift that evening. When Scott and Dawn finally locked up the building, they saw lights go back on inside the second-floor office. At this point, they were not going back inside.

Anna was standing in the lounge, waiting for the coffee to finish brewing, when she heard someone beside her sigh loudly. She looked over to acknowledge the person, but no one was there. She turned around looking from side to side, but no one else was in the lounge. This has happened to me a few times in the same lounge as well.

The employees in the depot have met Avery, a precocious and adorable three-year-old girl. Avery happens to be a medium—she sees dead people. Her brother Calvin, who is six years old, has psychic visions. There are many documented cases where these gifts are passed down through the generations, and this is one of those cases.

Avery began telling her grandparents that there was a man outside the sliding glass window at their home. She kept pointing him out. Her grandmother Sylvia closed the curtains, but this did not dissuade Avery, as she continued speaking of the man. That evening, Sylvia was a bit melancholy, as this was the anniversary of her father's death. She pulled out an old photo of her father and was reminiscing. Avery walked over, saw the photo and exclaimed, "That's the man I saw!"

When Avery visits the depot, she encounters many spirits, and she tells us all about them. One day, Avery and Sylvia were in the stairwell when she said to Sylvia, "Hey, where'd the man go?" Sylvia knew there hadn't been any man on the stairs, but Avery insisted he had been there. Avery looked up and down; she went to the closet at the stairs landing and looked inside. She was determined to find him despite her grandmother telling her no one had been there. Avery was upset that he was gone.

Avery also chatters about a different man and his dog that she frequently sees in the depot lobby. It's interesting that another adult woman saw an apparition of the man and the dog as well. Avery is frequently heard speaking to a young girl named Rosie at the depot. Over the past several years or so, we have shared numerous instances where people have had interactions with child spirits in the building. At least a dozen witnesses, adults and children alike, have heard these spirit children laughing and have even seen their apparitions.

One of the first indications the family had about Avery's brother Calvin's ability came when they were driving on Interstate 25 up near Douglas, Wyoming. Calvin was three years old at the time. He was napping in his car seat when, suddenly, he awoke, screaming frantically. His grandparents pulled the car over, but they could not get him to calm down. This young child was vividly describing the car accident his father, Jim, had when he was just eighteen years old, long before Calvin was born. What chilled his grandparents is that they were parked exactly where their son Jim's car had veered off the interstate all those years ago.

Sylvia grew up in Montana. As a child, she had many dreams about a green two-story house near her own home. In reality, there was just a pasture where she dreamed of the house. Sylvia recently learned that her grandparents had lived in a green two-story house on their land, just where she had dreamed it was. The home had been moved into town before Sylvia was born.

# TIVOLI

The Tivoli building is an elaborate, historic building that is featured on the cover of my *Haunted Cheyenne* book, and it is one of the most admired in town. It opened in 1893 as a fine restaurant, saloon and beer garden with working girls upstairs.

I presented ghost story walking tours during the Cheyenne Zombie Fest in September 2016. The groups walked around downtown and listened to stories. After the tour, a participant showed me a photo that he had taken of the Tivoli building during our walk. There was a woman's face and body in the first window beside the turret, although the building was vacant and locked up tight. There have been many sightings of this Victorian woman in the Tivoli by both employees and customers. Her essence is embedded into the building.

# MURRAY BUILDING

Ethereal images are painted on the side of the historic Murray Building. In 2001, the Murrays had the side of their three-story brick business

The cherub mural painted on the Murray Building in 2011 by Michael Cooper of Franklin, Tennessee.

building painted with a forty-foot-by-sixty-foot mural of a Renaissance cherub to convey a message of love, peace and understanding to the community. They had the building blessed once the painting was revealed.

An employee spoke of how wonderful it was to work there. She did say that there was something otherworldly in the building. The staff never feel alone when they are in the stairwell. There is a big room filled with pillows for the staff to relax or brainstorm. When the janitors clean the room, they stack up all the pillows so they can run the vacuum. One janitor slipped out of the room for a brief moment after stacking the pillows, and then she came back in to find them scattered all about the empty room. She left the building, retrieved her husband and made him go back into the building with her to finish her duties.

## DINNEEN BUILDING

According to the first Cheyenne City Directory, published in 1868, the first wooden structure in town was a private residence built by William

Dinneen Building, 2020.

Lorimer on the south bank of Crow Creek when Cheyenne was just eighteen days old. The first settler other than the Union Pacific's surveying crew is listed as James Whitehead, who set up his tent on Crow Creek on July 9, 1867, but others came later the same day. A few days later, the second wooden building, a saloon, went up at Lincolnway and Ferguson Street (now Carey Avenue). Before the end of the month, the two-story Whitehead Building had gone up a block west of the saloon at Lincolnway and Eddy (Pioneer Avenue). Within a month, there were more than five hundred settlers living on the prairie in wagons, tents and even dugouts. By the end of the summer, Cheyenne could boast four hundred structures scattered about.

Many Cheyenne history books say that the first building in town was the Whitehead Building, but the city directory of the time states differently. The first city council meetings were held on the second floor of the Whitehead Building. It was the first location of religious services in Cheyenne and where the vigilantes were said to meet. The buildings eventually became a row of secondhand stores. A June 19, 1912 *Wyoming Tribune* article stated that the city council voted to condemn the Whitehead block, as it was declared unsafe and unsanitary. It was razed in 1927, and Dinneen Lincoln Mercury was built in its place.

The Dinneen family operated the Bon-Ton Livery Stables. They consistently adjusted to Cheyenne's transportation needs over the decades, remaining open through 2006. The garage featured a water-operated hydraulic lift. Using fifty gallons of water, the pressure quietly raised cars from the first floor to the second floor, where many cars were stored. I read that during Prohibition, cars went up the water-powered lift, where it is said moonshine was removed from the spare gas tanks for distribution.[39]

In 2016, the esteemed Dinneen family received a Cheyenne Historic Preservation award for restoring and putting on a large addition to their Art Deco car dealership. They converted it into a restaurant and office space in 2011.

Today, there are offices on the upper floor. A lady who works there recently told me that a co-worker has experienced frequent interactions with a spirit that sweeps up her hair at the back of her neck. She feels a lot of taps and nudges from the spirit. Others have noticed things like the hand dryer in the restroom going off by itself.

# Move!

I met Ed when he used to do some maintenance in the depot building where I work. He was a man's man and didn't like to admit to believing in things that were out of the box. However, one day when I was working on the ghost tours, he saw some of my documents spread across my desk. His curiosity got the best of him, and he asked what I was working on. When I first told him, he acted like it was crazy stuff, but then after a year or so and a few conversations on the subject, he shared some stories with me.

Ed told of a time when he was living and working in San Diego. He had never believed in anything paranormal, but he heard this loud voice in his head saying, "Move your truck now!" He thought it strange, but he moved the truck. As soon as he moved it, a large boulder crashed down exactly where he had been parked. He would have been mortally wounded had he not heeded the otherworldly message.

Burke Senior Center.

## BURKE SENIOR CENTER

Nick, a phone technician, was programming a system at the Cheyenne Senior Center on O'Neil Avenue. There seemed to be something interfering with his efforts. The system was actually programming itself. Nick called the office and described what was occurring, but they told him that was impossible. He unplugged the phone and reconnected it, but the memory was completely erased, which is not supposed to happen. Every time he set his tools down, they were moved when he reached for them. This went on for days. Finally, he yelled at the ghost, and the system began to work; to his dismay, as he went on to a new job, the ghost actually followed him. Frustrated, Nick spoke out loud to the ghost, saying "Fine, if you want to work with me that's just great, but you need to follow directions. These people count on their phones, so just do what I tell you." He continued to have problems. He cursed at his new apprentice, and all the books on the shelf next to him fell to the floor. Nick was really annoyed, but that was the end of the ghostly assistance.

## SHOW TUNES AT THE ATLAS THEATRE

Tony's daughter is a member of the Paranormal Hunting Observation Group. One September day, he went with PHOG to the Atlas Theatre when they were preparing for the Cheyenne Zombie Fest. The team was near the stage. Tony wandered up to the second and third floors to check out the architecture; up there he heard a woman singing 1920s music. When he returned to the stage, he asked Jose if they had been playing any music. Jose had turned on Metallica for a minute, but not any show tunes.

PHOG had some candlesticks that were battery operated sitting on the stage for the presentation. Every time the members turned them off, they would turn back on.

A member of the melodrama theater group relayed some experiences he had at the theater. He said that he has felt spirits messing with his hair; they lightly tug at his hair and tickled his head. He said he has heard of many audience members experiencing this as well. A woman I met told me that she and her twelve-year-old daughter were sitting at a table in the theater eating their sandwiches when her daughter said, "Ow! My hair was just pulled!" The mother stood up and inspected to see if her daughter's hair was caught in the chair or anything, but it wasn't.

# WELLS FARGO

In 1882, five prominent cattle barons started the Wyoming Stock Growers Bank. In 1906, they erected a building at the corner of Seventeenth Street and Capitol Avenue. This building became the Wells Fargo Bank of Wyoming nearly a century later in 1998. The original stock growers bank walls remain underneath the building's façade. In the early days, there was a room where the "good ol' boys" hung out to iron out deals, gamble and drink. Today, people frequently smell tobacco smoke lingering in that room.

The bank tellers have experienced a variety of activity. Two of the women were in the ladies' room when one of the stall doors abruptly swung open, hitting the wall.

Leonard, a financial advisor, has encountered spirits at the bank; he says many employees have. There is a young girl spirit that appears on the second floor—he described her as playful. One evening, he was the only employee remaining at the bank. He was writing financial plans when the door chimes rang out. He looked up, but no one had entered through the locked doors. Leonard walked over and inspected the chime system. He cleaned the sensor and checked the battery. All appeared to be fine, so he returned to his desk. As soon as he settled in, the chimes rang out again. Aware of spirit activity in the building, he said, "Very funny" out loud. Then the chime went off repeatedly.

One afternoon, Tracy went down to the basement and was caught by surprise when she saw two children down there. She followed after them and called out. They vanished. She trudged back upstairs, feeling dumfounded. Tracy asked the other employees if anyone had their kids or grandkids at the bank. Everyone said no.

In the 1950s, there was a restaurant where the bank drive-up is today. Inside, a young airman from the base was quietly eating his meal. A man sitting in the adjoining booth suddenly turned and said, "You're fooling around with my wife, and I don't appreciate it. I'm going to kill you!" The flushed airman saw that the man had a pistol. He ran out of the restaurant, with the angry husband hot on his heels. A pistol shot rang out, and the airman fell dead. With all of the history of this bank, one can only speculate if this is the spirit responsible for some of the activity at the bank.

## WHISPER TO ME SOFTLY

Shelly works in a federal building on Capitol Avenue. When she or her co-workers are there alone on the weekend, they watch in wonder as the office doors open and close on their own. What intimidates her most is when she hears a man's voice beckoning her. He speaks her name aloud in the ladies' room, but she sees no one in the room or in the hall outside the restroom. "Shelly...Shelly...Shelleeeey."

## HOLY MOLY

Mary said she has worked for the First United Methodist Church for many years. The church is located downtown at East Eighteenth Street and Central Avenue.

Mary was there at 3:00 a.m. one night preparing for an event, and she kept hearing a door slam. "Hello?" she called out. But she didn't get any response. Full of anxiety, she walked around looking but found no

First United Methodist Church, Cheyenne, Wyoming. Carol M. Highsmith (1946–), photographer. *Carol M. Highsmith Archive, Library of Congress.*

one. The slamming resumed, and she left in a frenzy. Once the sun came up, Mary went back to the church to finish up. She walked past a photo of a former member they all fondly called "Uncle French." She noticed something on the floor and picked up a nametag that read "Norm French." As other church employees filtered in and saw the nametag on Mary's desk, they were all saying, "Where in the world did you get that?" and were astonished when she showed them where she found it. The nametag had been put in a box and packed away ten years ago. No one had seen it in years. They decided maybe Norm wanted his photo to be labeled, so they hung his nametag with the photo.

Another night, Mary was there with the janitor when a door began to bang. He said, "Who is here?" Mary said, "No one. That is Norm." He didn't believe her, and the door banged a few more times. He searched the entire place and checked that all exterior doors were locked. He returned, shaking his head.

## DAVIS BUILDING

The Davis Building has housed different rehabilitation facilities over the years. In the 1990s, it held residents who were mentally disabled. On the third floor was a juvenile program for runaway and troubled children. Because of the nature of this facility, the building was locked down with high security. One night, around 11:00 p.m., the police brought a new girl in. During the "intake" process, they always took a Polaroid picture for the file. Peggy had this teenage girl stand in the center of the hallway and snapped the picture. She was interviewing the girl while another staff member was processing her paperwork. The second staff person began tugging on Peggy's arm, pointing at the picture. There was a clear image of a man in the air above the girl. His whole figure could be seen except for his feet. He wore a hat and a vintage suit that Peggy described as a zoot suit.

Davis Building on Eighteenth Street. Once a grocery store, it houses the Cheyenne Transitional Center today.

Peggy took the Polaroid to the staff meeting in the morning so that the rest of the employees could view the apparition. All were amazed, even though the residents often reported seeing a man in the hall. Prior to this event, there was often talk of the building being haunted. They called him the "Goodwill Ghost."

The staff could not figure out why the elevator would frequently go up by itself when all residents were sound asleep. When the doors opened, no one would be on the elevator. They would also hear the sounds of the office and sleeping room doors open and close, but their security checks would not find anything.

# Fowlers (Z's)

In April 2019, the City of Cheyenne tore down the old Carey Building, along with its 142 years of history.

Roedel's Drug Store was located in the Carey Building. Mr. Roedel collected water in a bucket in his basement from condensation dripping from steam heat pipes. He then sold it as distilled water. Druggists were not regulated in any way and were making their own concoctions to treat people. It was trial and error. Sometimes they stumbled on something effective, but one could never be sure if it would cure or kill them. Roedel must have done things right because his store operated successfully for 117 years. He was the first man in Wyoming to hold a pharmacist license. Roedel's Drug Store opened in 1889 and was the oldest operating business in Cheyenne, closing its doors in 2007, although it had moved the store a few blocks north on Carey Avenue.

Most Cheyenne residents know it as the Fowlers Department Store and then Z's Home Furnishings. I worked for Fowlers when I was in high school. The building had really been neglected over the years, but I still felt a bit nostalgic about it. Construction has begun on a new city municipal facility.

A former employee at Z's Home Furnishings told me several years ago that four of the employees he'd worked with all believed there was something supernatural in a mirror. They refused to go to the downstairs level. To further their concerns, the Z's employees also witnessed chairs rocking of their own accord in the break room. I wonder where these spirits are today.

## CHAPLIN SCHOOL

Park Addition School opened at 1100 Richardson Court in Cheyenne in 1921. It was quite small, so in 1945, they added onto the school and changed the name to Chaplin School, honoring longtime teacher Ruth Chaplin. The school was used for classes until 1956. At that time, they moved into the new Pioneer Park School. The Chaplin Building was used for school administration offices until it was sold in 1977. A daycare was there for a number of years.[40] Some young explorers snuck into the abandoned school and captured an interesting piece of audio here. They reported sightings of a ghost in the principal's window and moaning sounds in a classroom. On the audio they captured, I heard a child's voice saying, "Get it." The voice is distinctly different from that of the youngsters.

## PLAINS HOTEL

The Plains Hotel has been a fixture on Lincolnway Street since 1911. Lincolnway is a section of the old Lincoln Highway and is the main street going through downtown Cheyenne. There are many experiences recounted in my *Haunted Cheyenne* book—here are a few more.

I came across a Trip Advisor review exclaiming that the Plains Hotel is haunted. It was written by a business traveler who had stayed at the hotel for three weeks. He said that he was continually getting tapped and poked on the shoulders, and he felt like he was being watched. He would hear laughter, sighs and the word *hey* all up close in his ear from an unseen source. He claimed that he even saw a few shadowy ghosts. He ended his review by saying it is a great place to stay!

One afternoon, my friend Dori, who is a psychic medium, was walking down the hallway of the fifth floor of the Plains Hotel. She passed a gentleman, who said, "Good afternoon ma'am," as he tipped his hat. She responded in kind and then got a feeling; she turned, and the man had vanished. She realized that his clothing had been that of a different era. Later, when she was on the main floor, she noticed a historic photo from a 1912 cattlemen's convention that was hanging up. In the photo, she saw the same man in the picture that had greeted her in the hall. Dori said that photos can throw out energy. Sometimes the energy given off affects your comfort level.

Side view of the Historic Plains Hotel on Central Avenue. It opened in 1911.

In September 2016, we held the Rocky Mountain Spirits Paranormal Convention at the Plains Hotel. There were psychic mediums, ghost investigators and even a shaman presenting at the conference. Erica, a psychic medium, did readings all day. Feeling fatigued, she took refuge in her room around midnight. She had no interest in communicating with the other side, since she had done it all day long.

Erica lay on top of her bed and turned the TV on. Then she noticed a shaking noise. She ignored it, thinking that it was something in the hotel or one of the neighboring guests. As she watched the television, the sound continued.

About an hour later, she reached for her water bottle and realized the bottle was shaking rather fiercely. Then she noticed the entire bedside table was shaking intensely. Right then, she got a psychic image of a cowboy in her head, an older man with gray hair; he seemed exhausted. She reached over, touched the bedside table and said, "You need to stop." The table stopped shaking altogether. It started up again later, so she said, "Cut it out," and it stopped again.

Erica turned off the lights, snuggled under the covers and was just falling asleep when she felt something lean against the bed. The mattress was pushed hard enough to make the bed tilt. Erica sat up, turned on the light and firmly said, "Okay, you need to leave until I'm gone tomorrow." She had no other issues the rest of the night.

There have been other sightings of a cowboy spirit at the Plains Hotel. In 2013, Christy told us of an evening when she was having dinner with her friend Sue at the hotel restaurant. At one point, Sue's face turned to stone. Christy actually feared that she was suffering a stroke. Alarmed, she grabbed Sue's arm, saying, "Are you ok?" Sue asked if she had seen the cowboy that just walked past them. He was translucent. Guests have commented on waking up to find a cowboy sitting on their bed, but then he vanishes before them.

There is an old photo taken in the Plains Hotel bar many years ago. It hangs in the Wig Wam room at the hotel, which is the old bar. In the photo, there is not anyone standing at the bar, but when you look at the mirrored bar back, you see the images of five men in the mirror bellied up to the bar. This gives us a peek into the past. Stop in and check it out.

# CHEEK TO CHEEK: HOUSE OF MIRRORS

Cheeks International Academy of Beauty stands at the same location of what once was Ida Hamilton's House of Mirrors, the biggest brothel ever operated in Wyoming and certainly the finest, most lavish brothel found in Cheyenne. There were colossal floor-to-ceiling mirrors in the foyer, giving the house its name. Engraved invitations were sent to the region's prominent men for opening night. Next door was the Double Decker, a less pretentious brothel.[41] This is in downtown Cheyenne, Wyoming, on the West 200 block of Seventeenth Street.

In Cheyenne's early rough and rowdy years, characters with varied moral standards were required to cohabitate with one another. Three of the four street corners of this same block were occupied by churches. An exclusive housing structure called Maple Terrace stood across the street from the brothels. An odd mixture of folks, to be sure.

Madame Ida retired as a very well-to-do woman in the mid-1880s, at which time the building served as Yee Jim's Laundry, washing away the sins of the building. Later, it was a hospital and rooming house. The building was torn down after sixty years, and a blond brick building was constructed in 1942. Cheyenne Bowling Lanes was listed in the city directories there in the 1950s.

Cheeks Beauty Academy, formerly a bowling alley. This is the location where Ida Hamilton's House of Mirrors stood in the 1880s.

Now we have the cutting-edge Cheeks Academy, where members of staff encounter a playful spirit. Her tall silhouette is often seen, although when they try to focus their eyes on her, she vanishes before them. A few psychics have come into the academy; they have all said the spirit is that of a cocktail waitress who worked at the bowling lanes. Whether it is the cocktail waitress or one of Ida's shady ladies, the staff experiences a lot of paranormal activity in the back hallway by the alley door and in the laundry room. A few years ago, the dryer kept turning off in the middle of drying towels. They replaced the dryer, and the new dryer turned off too—off and on, off and on. Often times, articles like their combs and brushes come up missing, and then they are found again in extremely strange places.

Selina was doing the normal closing routine one day. Starting at the back of the school, she locked the back door. Working her way forward, she made sure all the lights, curling irons and appliances were off. When she got to the front door, she turned around to survey the room. The lights started turning back on, one by one

Maddie, an instructor, said that when everybody leaves and the radio is turned off, she hears spellbinding notes of jewelry box music flowing through the air.

# DAN D RENTAL

Dan D Rental is located on Storey Boulevard in Cheyenne. I was told of typical ghostly happenings such as objects being moved when no one is looking and lights turning on and off by themselves at this business.

Liz was locking up the store for the night. She turned the key in the door and heard the *click*, and when she turned around, there was a bald man in his twenties standing behind the counter. Liz apologized to the man with a mysterious air, saying, "I'm so sorry. I thought all our customers had left. I'll let you out." She turned slightly to unlock the door, but as she looked back toward the counter, the man was gone. Her eyes swept across the room, finding no one. She wandered throughout the entire store, checking every nook and cranny, concerned about being locked in the store with a stranger, but finally she determined that she was alone. The man had looked very real, which is why she spoke to him, and then he was just gone.

# WYOMING NATIONAL GUARD MUSEUM

The Wyoming National Guard Museum on Pershing Boulevard has an active spirit or two. One day, when Bob was volunteering, he heard all the cupboards in the adjoining room slam, one after another. He thought it was a colleague and shouted out, "Cool your jets, Barney!" But when he entered the room, it was empty. Perplexed, he went back to his project, and twenty minutes later, the cupboards slammed again. Bob said that when the staff are there at night, they often hear imposing footsteps from overhead and jumbled voices, but then they are sitting beside two cemeteries, after all.

# TRAFFIC SAFETY SERVICES

Two local Cheyenne men who work for Traffic Safety Services were picking up safety signs that were to be set up for traffic control. They went to pick these signs up at two o'clock in the morning because everything needed to placed on the roads by six o'clock the following morning before people headed to work. The warehouse where the signs are kept is located on North American Road.

When the men arrived at the warehouse, they got out of their vehicle and parked on the west side of the building. They were loading traffic cones into their truck under the moon beams when they heard a large overhead garage door roll open. They looked around, but no one was there and the garage door to the warehouse was closed. Confused, they looked at each other, questioning who else would be out there at that hour. The garage door to the warehouse was closed. Then they heard a man's voice from right beside them say, "Oh hey," followed by the rolling sound of a large overhead door closing, but again they saw no one. The pair walked around the entire building, but no one was out there besides the two of them.

CHAPTER 17

# HOSPITALS

## DePaul Hospital

It stands to reason that some spirits would remain at hospitals. DePaul Catholic Hospital was on the east side of town. Opening in 1952, it was operated by the Sisters of Charity of Leavenworth. Today, the facility houses United Regional Medical Center Rehabilitation and Behavioral Health Units.

A former nurse told of a young boy spirit that was frequently observed in red overalls up on the third floor. They called him Eric. The spirits of a nun and of a priest were also seen often. There was lots of activity on the fifth floor, where the nuns used to live. I asked other former DePaul nurses about ghosts. They remembered that during a big remodel in the late 1970s, there was talk that the spirit of a nun was seen by the construction workers. The fifth floor had a hospice room that had been reserved for nuns who chose to remain at DePaul during their final earthly days, and several sisters died there. I believe they visit and continue to be caregivers at the hospital.

## Hospital Building

There used to be a small brick building to the west of the Cheyenne Regional Medical Center Emergency Room that was used for the hospital foundation offices. They tore it down for new hospital buildings and an ER expansion.

Katie worked here for many years and claimed that she worked with a ghost. She and others felt it was a female spirit. When working upstairs alone, Katie would hear the front door open. She would go down to greet whoever was coming in but find no one. Hesitantly, she'd go back up to her desk, knowing that she would hear someone on the stairs. Heart pounding, she would go investigate but find no one. Shortly after sitting back down, she would be encompassed by a bone-chilling draft. The director asked the spirits out loud to leave the employees alone. He said that was a first in his experience as director.

# Cheyenne Veterans Administration Hospital

The Cheyenne Veterans Hospital construction was completed in 1934, but the property has undergone many changes over the years.[42]

In the Arrowhead Building, the paper towels feed out by themselves, and unattended toilets flush. Random footsteps are heard when no one is seen.

I have a treasured friendship with Jose Gonzales, who works as a respiratory therapist at the VA Hospital. We first met when I invited Paranormal Hunters Observation Group to be a part of the trolley Halloween tours. Jose's interest in the paranormal began as a child, when they had a frightening presence in their home. His story is included in my *Haunted Cheyenne* book. He had a unique upbringing, as his grandfather was a Yaqui shaman in northern Mexico, while the other side of his family was strict Catholic.

One of Jose's co-workers and friends at the Veterans Administration Hospital in Cheyenne passed away in 2010. One day, Jose was with a patient when the phone in the exam room rang. Jose answered it, and it was a doctor who was wondering why Jose had just called him. Jose said he hadn't called because he was with a patient. The doctor insisted that the call had come from that extension. As soon as Jose was done with the patient, he stepped into the hall, where he saw the apparition of his deceased colleague. He knew that his friend was responsible for the phone tag.

I engaged in a Facebook conversation with a VA employee after reading her comment mentioning that the ghosts had "really been at it the past two nights." After some correspondence, I learned that one of her colleagues had noticed a little boy out of the corner of her eye. It was late, and she knew there were no children in the facility at that hour. Nervously, she looked straight on, expecting him to disappear, but he just sat there. She said he was not a solid human form, but rather somewhat transparent. She broke out in a sweat and began shaking. The nurse call buttons went off continuously throughout the night, but when they checked on the patients, they were found sound asleep. One patient screamed out. The nurse rushed to his room, where he was anxiously pointing and was quite hysterical about the apparition he had seen. The patient made them look under his bed and in the closets before leaving him. He did not want to stay in the room.

There are a number of staff members who have witnessed an apparition in the men's restroom in the Veterans Benefits Administration section of the main hospital. He is dressed in slacks and a button-up shirt and appears to be middle age. His appearance has been independently corroborated by the different witnesses. It's unknown who he is, whether a former employee or a veteran who passed at the hospital. Most folks lean toward it being a veteran who passed, considering how close the Veterans Benefits area is to the nursing home section of the hospital.

A security man reported regularly seeing an elderly gentlemen in the Circle of Flags area late at night. Of course, the residents of the nursing home aren't allowed to be outside the building at night, let alone by themselves. Security staff would approach the man, and he would disappear when their vehicles got close. The sighting was so frequent that they quit approaching the apparition, knowing that it would disperse.

## WARREN AIR FORCE BASE HOSPITAL

Annie worked as a nurse at the base hospital in the 1990s. This incident happened right before it closed and was changed to clinic services only on the base. Annie worked the OB ward. She said there weren't any patients on this particular night, which really wasn't unusual. There were three nurses and two emergency room techs on duty. The three nurses were sitting together chatting when they heard a baby cry. All of them got up thinking a new patient had come in, but there was no one. The two emergency techs also heard the crying. They searched the entire hospital, including closets and the basement. All five of them distinctly heard the crying baby for a half an hour before the wailing ceased.

# CONCLUSION

*Still round the corner there may wait/A new road or a secret gate/And though I oft have passed them by a day will come at last when I shall take the hidden paths that run West of the Moon, East of the Sun.*
*—J.R.R. Tolkien*

People who experience a spirit are often frightened due the shock of the experience, but more often than not the spirit's intent is not malicious or dark. If the person stood back and was open minded to the experience, they may realize that it was a positive interaction.

My goal with this book is to help people realize that there is another dimension that we transition into when our spirit leaves this world. There is no reason to be afraid of dying. Our loved ones are still around us on a daily basis. Although it's hard when we cannot physically hear, see or touch them, all the instances in the book prove that they do try to let us know they are still with us, and they guide us in our earthly endeavors. Watch for their subtle messages.

When our time comes to cross over, we can expect to see the family and friends we have missed so much along with our spirit guides—all there to greet and embrace us. It is my hope that this compilation of people's experiences can help to ease any fears and concerns that you hold. Just embrace universal love.

# NOTES

## Introduction

1. Before It's News, "Scientist Photographs the Soul Leaving the Body," September 25, 2013, https://beforeitsnews.com/beyond-science/2013/09/scientist-photographs-the-soul-leaving-the-body-2443674.html; Leonard George, PhD, *Alternate Realities: The Paranormal, the Mystic and the Transcendent in Human Experience* (N.p.: Facts on File Inc., n.d.), 119.

## Part I

2. History Channel, *Joan of Arc*, A&E Television, November 2009, https://www.history.com/topics/middle-ages/saint-joan-of-arc; Yvonne Lanhers and Malcolm G.A. Vale, "St. Joan of Arc: French Heroine," Britannica, https://www.britannica.com/biography/Saint-Joan-of-Arc, last updated May 26, 2020.
3. History Disclosure Team, "Abraham Lincoln Had a Precognitive Dream Before His Assassination," February 21, 2017, https://www.historydisclosure.com/lincoln-had-a-precognitive-dream; Beth Scott and Michael Norman, *Haunted America*, vol. 1 (N.p.: Tom Doherty Association, 2007), 69.

## *Part II*

4. National Register of Historic Places.

5. Ibid.

6. Lori Van Pelt, *Capitol Characters of Cheyenne*, Series: Dreamers & Schemers, Book 2, 1st ed. (N.p.: High Plains Press, 2006), 234–39; Martha Thompson, "Daze's Long Exciting Life Has Become Legend in Cheyenne," *Wyoming Tribune Eagle*, May 15, 1988.

7. Van Pelt, *Capitol Characters of Cheyenne*; Thompson, "Daze's Long Exciting Life."

8. Wyoming State Archives, "The Annals of Wyoming," 1:1, 2:19, 1:3:20, 2:4:78, 6:4:324 and 7:1:364.

9. National Register of Historic Places.

10. Wyoming State Archives, "Annals of Wyoming."

11. Thompson, "Daze's Long Exciting Life."

12. Van Pelt, *Capitol Characters of Cheyenne*.

13. Thompson, "Daze's Long Exciting Life"; Wyoming State Archives, "Annals of Wyoming."

14. Van Pelt, *Capitol Characters of Cheyenne*.

15. *New York Times*, "Ali McGraw [*sic*] Is the Bride of Steve McQueen in West," July 13, 1973, https://www.nytimes.com/1973/07/13/archives/ali-mcgraw-is-the-bride-of-steve-mcqueen-in-west.html.

16. Before It's News, "Scientist Photographs the Soul Leaving the Body"; *Wyoming Blue Book*, vol. 4 (Cheyenne: Wyoming State Archives, 1990), 393.

17. Judith Adams, *Cheyenne City of Blue Sky* (N.p.: Windsor Publications, 1988), 53, 93.

18. National Register of Historic Places.

19. Ibid.

20. Bill O'Neal, *A Biography of the Magic City of the Plains*, 1st ed. (Fort Worth, TX: Eakin Press, 2006), 102, 137, 157–58, 179; Open Jurist, "John Alder Riner," https://openjurist.org/judge/john-alden-riner.

21. National Register of Historic Places; *Wyoming Blue Book*, vol. 4.

22. Find A Grave, "Edwin J. Smalley," https://www.findagrave.com/memorial/29170126/edwin-john-smalley.

23. *Wyoming Blue Book*, vol. 4.

24. *New York Times*, Edd Bailey Obituary, September 13, 1988, https://www.nytimes.com/1988/09/13/obituaries/edd-bailey-dies-at-83-once-headed-railroad.html; Find A Grave, "Luke Vorhees," https://www.findagrave.com/memorial/29171396/luke-voorhees; "Today in Old West History."

25. *Wyoming Blue Book*, vol. 4.

26. National Register of Historic Places.

27. *Wyoming Blue Book*, vol. 4.

28. O'Neal, *Biography of the Magic City of the Plains*; Marie Miller, "Laramie County, Wyoming," Genealogy Trails, from *Progressive Men of the State of Wyoming* (N.p.: A.W. Bowen & Company, 1901), http://genealogytrails.com/wyo/laramie/laramiecountybiosrw.html.

## *Part III*

29. National Register of Historic Places.

30. Ibid.

31. Ibid.

32. Ibid.

33. Ibid.

34. Wyoming State Historical Society, Laramie County Chapter, "Cheyenne Landmarks," 1976, 25, 71.

35. National Register of Historic Places.

36. Ibid.

37. Ibid.

38. O'Neal, *Biography of the Magic City of the Plains*; Miller, "Laramie County, Wyoming"; "Today in Old West History."

39. Jodi Rogstad, "Final Cut at Rube's Masonic Temple Barbershop," *Wyoming Tribune Eagle*, July 4, 2009, http://www.wyomingnews.com/articles/2009/07/04/featured_story/01top_07-04-09.txt.

40. Adams, *Cheyenne City of Blue Sky*.

41. O'Neal, *Biography of the Magic City of the Plains*.

42. National Register of Historic Places.

# ABOUT THE AUTHOR

Jill Pope has written two previous books on the paranormal, *Haunted Cheyenne* and *Haunted Warren Air Force Base*. In her tourism position as director of operations for Visit Cheyenne and the Cheyenne Street Railway, Jill has written more than thirty paranormal trolley tour scripts, so her catalogue of stories is quite extensive. She has presented on the paranormal several times and has hosted a few paranormal workshops and events in Cheyenne, including the 2016 Spirit Spree. Besides being an author and tourism expert, Jill is also an artist, having worked in paints and pastels, and she has sculpted bronze statues. She has painted three public art eight-foot-tall cowboy boots. Jill is a wife, the mother of five and the grandmother of five, along with being a pet mom of two Westies and a Kunekune house pig. She is excited to publish this book on the positive side of paranormal experiences.